A GOSPEL PRIMER
FOR CHRISTIANS

Gospel. *n.* (*god*, good + *spel*, news) good news of salvation for hell-deserving sinners through the Person and work of Jesus Christ.

Primer. *n.* a book that covers the basic elements of a subject.

Milton Vincent

A Gospel Primer for Christians
by Milton Vincent

"...the gospel....
...of first importance..."

1 Corinthians 15:1,3

"If there's anything in life that we should be passionate about, it's the gospel. And I don't mean passionate only about sharing it with others. I mean passionate about thinking about it, dwelling on it, rejoicing in it, allowing it to color the way we look at the world. Only one thing can be of first importance to each of us. And only the gospel ought to be."

C.J. Mahaney, *The Cross Centered Life*, 20-21

"Many Christians think the gospel is only for unbelievers. Milton Vincent learned the hard way that we Christians also need the gospel every day to keep us from falling into a performance relationship with God. I share Milton's enthusiasm for the gospel and warmly commend his 'primer' to all believers. It can literally be life changing."

Jerry Bridges, author of *The Discipline of Grace* and *The Gospel for Real Life*

"As a pastor, I've observed many Christians who are grateful for the gospel but have difficulty applying the gospel to their lives. The truth is, I need to preach the gospel to myself every day-and you do too! In *A Gospel Primer for Christians* Milton Vincent has created a practical tool with a powerful effect. This book will help you understand the gospel more profoundly, reflect on the gospel more faithfully, and experience the power of the gospel more consistently."

C.J. Mahaney, President, Sovereign Grace Ministries, and author of *The Cross-Centered Life*

"My good friend and fellow pastor, Milton Vincent, is utterly obsessed with the gospel of Jesus Christ. In *A Gospel Primer for Christians*, he demonstrates why believers–even though already having become the recipients of God's saving love–ought nevertheless to be continually infatuated with this glorious reality. His capturing of the doctrine of salvation is unique in that virtually every section is explicitly footnoted to multiple Scriptural passages. Part III of the book, with the gospel shown in a beautiful poetic narrative, is alone worth the price of the book. I know of no other book quite like it, both in its approach and impact."

Lance Quinn, Pastor-Teacher of The Bible Church of Little Rock, Little Rock, Arkansas

"Most Christians live on the porch of their faith without enjoying the mansion of delights behind the front door. In *A Gospel Primer for Christians*, Milton Vincent takes believers on an amazing tour of the gospel, showing how its familiar truths are actually its most overlooked treasures. This book will not only increase what you know about the gospel, but it will take what you know and helpfully show you what to do with it. This book has made me love the Savior more intimately, hate my sin more deeply, and find the joy that comes from gospel-produced holiness. Open its pages and enjoy the gospel's mansion of delights!"

> **Rick Holland**, Senior Associate Pastor, Grace Community Church, and Director of D.Min. Studies at The Master's Seminary

"There is no greater news than that Jesus came to die for our sins in order to bring us to God. This biblically saturated book will help you understand why that is such great news. Milton Vincent's *Gospel Primer for Christians* is one of the rare books that helps us not only to know the Gospel, but also to love the Gospel and see how it applies to every area of our lives. I have used the pre-published version of this book in my devotions for years and I'm thrilled that more people are now able to benefit from it."

> **Bob Kauflin**, Director of Worship Development, Sovereign Grace Ministries

"The exhortation to 'preach the gospel to yourself' is a clarion call in a vacuous time within evangelicalism. But what does it mean to 'preach the Gospel to oneself' and how can one practically do it? Milton, who obviously meditates on it himself, elaborates on this privilege and grace in such a way that the Christian can revel in God's grace and the person and work of Christ more intentionally. This book can help any Christian echo the words of the Baptist Preacher/Theologian Andrew Fuller, who said in his diary, 'Compared with what I deserve to be, how happy my condition!'"

> **Stuart Scott**, Associate Professor of Biblical Counseling, Southern Baptist Theological Seminary, and author of *The Exemplary Husband*

Dedication

To all
who have taught me,
and teach me still

Acknowledgments

So many have been instrumental to the development of this book, and some deserve special mention.

I am grateful to all those faithful souls at The Master's Seminary, Bob Jones University, and the churches I've attended throughout my life who have taught me and brought me along in my understanding of God and His Word. This book is a tribute to all of them.

Thanks should go to my parents, Bill and Janie Vincent, for teaching me from childhood the Holy Scriptures, within which I have found that which is "*of first importance.*"

A special thanks goes to Ib and Yrsa Hansen. Ib managed the internet presentation and distribution of the pre-published primer and also skillfully rescued the electronic copy of the primer from my crashed computer the week I was to send the copy to the publisher. Yrsa handled virtually all the distribution for the pre-published edition of this book and managed the editorial team. I am deeply grateful to both of them for their devotion to this project.

I am much indebted to my younger brother, Robert Vincent, who always so willingly read and offered feedback on every aspect of this primer (from cover to cover) as it developed over the last two and a half years.

Thanks also goes to Ruby Kimble, Cindy Bendshadler, Terrie van Baarsel, Kim Davis, Michelle Assaturian, Kathy Dane, Leah Simpson, Diane Swaim, and Metrice Rochowicz for their crucial work on the editorial team.

I am thankful also for Mike Bullmore and C.J. Mahaney, two new friends in the gospel, without whose feedback and encouragement this project would never have reached this juncture.

A huge thanks goes to my precious wife, Donna, for her undying love for me. Apart from her, some of the gospel truths in this book would never have been grasped by me. I thank God for her patience with me over the years as I have stumbled towards an understanding of the gospel and for her willingness to join me in believing its glorious truths.

I should also give thanks for my four children: Brooke, Brendan, Benjamin, and Breanna. I deserve wrath, yet instead God gives me them. Wow! Through them I have tasted the unconditionality of God's good favor, and I pray that they have tasted that gracious favor in return. I am grateful for their endurance of my obsessive preoccupations with readying this book for publication and for their many encouragements along the way.

My gratitude also goes out to Jan Haley, President of Focus Publishing, who contacted me expressing an interest in publishing this book. It is, indeed, a gracious providence that our paths have crossed on this project, and she truly has been a blessing to work with. I am thankful for Barbara VanThomma's work on the beautiful cover design and for Melanie Schmidt's painstaking work of reformatting and editing this work for publication.

I must also thank the elders and congregation of Cornerstone Fellowship Bible Church, whose love for God and for me has always created a climate in which I could learn God's truth and preach it with liberty Sunday after Sunday. They have grown along with me these last sixteen years and have shown me first-hand the power and glory of the gospel.

Most importantly, I am thankful to my Heavenly Father for sending His Son into the world so that my salvation might be accomplished, to Jesus for giving Himself over in death for me, and to the Holy Spirit for opening my eyes to the glory of the gospel. May He, the Triune God, find this book a serviceable tool to advance His glory.

Contents

Foreword
by Mike Bullmore

I believe I was born again when I was eight. I was sitting under the preaching of a godly British missionary named Derek Porter. He was preaching from the book of Jonah about God's grace toward sinners. God used that preaching to speak both deep conviction and wonderful hope to my soul. Later that evening, my father alongside me, I confessed my sinfulness to God and asked him to save me from my sin and all its consequences and to give me the gift of new life in Christ. That is, I believe, when I was born again.

But it wasn't until my mid-twenties that I came to have what I would consider a deep personal understanding and a deep personal treasuring of the gospel. I had been living for years with a heart marked by pride. God patiently but persistently resisted that pride until it broke. And in the wake of that breaking a new kind of understanding took root. It felt like another conversion. A great awakening.

In the ensuing years God used many things to nurture this new working of the gospel: particularly, the preaching and writing of John Piper (which helped me to wonder at the sheer greatness of God revealed in and through the gospel), the friendship and counsel of C.J. Mahaney (which helped me to see the relevance of the gospel to every area of life), and the personal Spirit-directed ministry of my wife Beverly (which helps me know of God's personal favor toward me flowing out from the gospel).

And recently, God has been greatly using this book by Milton Vincent. I first read an early draft of this book back in the fall of 2005 on the way home from a conference at which I had met Milton. He had handed me a copy, humbly asking if I might read it and give him some feedback. I remember

3

being deeply affected over and over again on that plane ride home as I read Milton's "Reasons to Rehearse the Gospel Daily." It was clear these ideas had been born out of careful, loving, prayerful meditation on gospel truth and it was clear that they had taken time to form. They had a weight and a clarity and a beautiful precision about them. I felt like I had been given a handful of precious diamonds and I could not stop looking at them.

When I arrived at home I immediately emailed Vincent telling him of the effect of his book on my heart and asking him how I might get copies. (I was eager to put the *Primer* in the hands of all my fellow pastors, elders and the care group leaders at my church.) I also urged him to get the *Primer* published. I wanted others, many others, to benefit as I had. In the following months I found myself returning to the *Primer* over and over (in my personal devotions, in our life together as a pastoral team, in pastoral counseling) and I kept having Milton send me more and more copies for our church bookstore. You can imagine my delight when I got word that Focus Publishing had agreed to publish *A Gospel Primer*. I rejoice greatly in this!

This book was written slowly. It savors of a slow cooking. I believe it will be best read slowly. Take your time with it. Let its truths drip down deep. And return to it often. Let it regularly help you preach the life-giving, soul-reviving, heart-rejoicing gospel to yourself. Keep it close by your bed or the place of your time alone with God. It is, quite simply, one of the most spiritually useful books I've read.

Mike Bullmore
Preaching Pastor
CrossWay Community Church
Kenosha, Wisconsin

Introduction

This book is offered as a handy guide to help Christians experience the gospel more fully by preaching it to themselves each day. It is also offered as a correction to a costly mistake made by Christians who view the gospel as something that has fully served out its purpose the moment they believed in Jesus for salvation. Not knowing what to do with the gospel once they are saved, they lay it aside soon after conversion so they can move on to "bigger and better" things (even Scriptural things). Of course, they don't think this is what they are doing at the time, yet after many years of floundering in defeat they can look back and see that this is exactly what they have done.

God did not give us His gospel just so we could embrace it and be converted. Actually, He offers it to us every day as a gift that keeps on giving to us everything we need for life and godliness. The wise believer learns this truth early and becomes proficient in extracting available benefits from the gospel each day. We extract these benefits by being absorbed in the gospel, speaking it to ourselves when necessary, and by daring to reckon it true in all we do.

God's gifts are all of grace, and there is nothing we can do to earn them. However, the wise believer will make sure he is positioning himself in the spot where God's gracious gifts are located. And the Scripture teaches that all such gifts are located inside the gospel. Hence, the Bible tells Christians to be continuously established and steadfast in the gospel and to refuse to be moved from there (*Colossians 1:23*).

As for myself, after years of frustration, fits and starts, and exhausted collapses in my Christian walk, I have come back to a focus on the gospel and have found its sufficiency for daily living to be truly overwhelming. After years of church attendance, university and seminary training, and countless hours of Bible study in preparation for preaching many hundreds of sermons, I have found nothing more powerful and life-transforming than the gospel truths affirmed on the following pages. Rehearsing these truths each day has become a pleasurable discipline by which I enjoy God's love and maintain fresh contact with His provision and power for daily living.

Over the course of time, preaching the gospel to myself every day has made more of a difference in my life than any other discipline I have ever practiced. I find myself sinning less, but just as importantly, I find myself recovering my footing more quickly after sinning, due to the immediate comfort found in the gospel. I have also found that when I am absorbed in the gospel, everything else I am supposed to be toward God and others seems to flow out of me more naturally and passionately. Doing right is not always easy, but it is never more easy than when one is breathing deeply the atmosphere of the gospel. I am confident that you will find the same to be true in your life as well.

This book is written partly as a result of the influence of Jerry Bridges' excellent book entitled *The Discipline of Grace* (NavPress, 1994), for it was through this book that I first heard the challenge to preach the gospel to myself every day. Since that time, my method of rehearsing the gospel has evolved from a short list of gospel truths on a 3 x 5 card into the formats presented on the following pages. It is my hope that the formats below will be basic enough for the average reader, yet sufficiently thorough to cover the main categories of gospel thought.

The first part of this book contains *Reasons to Rehearse the Gospel Daily*. The thirty-one reasons given are designed to remind you, the reader, of some valuable blessings which the gospel can render in the life of the believer who rehearses the gospel in faith each day. The second and third parts of the book contain A Gospel Narrative in both a prose and poetic format respectively. Both formats are written in a way that facilitates memorization and smooth recital of the gospel. At the bottom of every page are relevant Scriptures that affirm the truths expressed.

Everything in sections I - III is written in the first person singular (I, my, me), for all that is said in these sections is your testimony if you are a believer in Jesus. Therefore, read these words, or better, speak them aloud as a way of testifying daily to your own heart the truth of what God has done for you and made available for you in the gospel. You'd be amazed at the difference such a practice can make in your life.

The last part of this book, entitled, Surprised by the Gospel, recounts a portion of my personal gospel testimony and also explains how this book came to be. My hope is that my story will encourage you in the gospel and also motivate you to write the story of your own experience of the gospel. You will find great value in rehearsing the details of your own personal gospel story, and others can receive huge blessing from it as well.

Please view this book as a primer of sorts, as a tool designed merely to get you launched in preaching the gospel to yourself and rehearsing its benefits. The precise wording in sections I - III need not be recited slavishly. In fact, over time you will likely develop your own wording and emphases as your proficiency in the gospel grows. Consequently, you may eventually reach a point where you no longer have need of this tool. If such a day comes, then the purpose of this book will have been fully served.

Also, as you are preaching the gospel to yourself, please savor the tender involvement of the Holy Spirit with you in the process. (Apart from Him, this discipline would be of no effect!) The gospel is true, but it is the Holy Spirit who makes it vivid to the soul. The gospel first came *"by the Holy Spirit sent from heaven"* (1 Peter 1:12); and as you preach the gospel to yourself in dependence upon Him, the gospel will come to you afresh by that same Holy Spirit. The Spirit will seize the opportunity to pour out God's love in your heart (Romans 5:5); and He will, through the gospel, disclose the heart of the Father towards you (John 16:14-15). Your heavenly Father knew that you would never comprehend on your own the depths of His love, so He sent His Spirit into your life so that the Spirit might search out the very depths of the love of God and then reveal such things to you (1 Corinthians 2:9-10,12). Certainly, the Spirit is ministering to you in this way at all times, but preaching the gospel to yourself provides an opportunity for the Spirit to do so in a concentrated fashion. Such a reality elevates this discipline beyond the mere recitation of facts into something that is profoundly personal between you and the Holy Spirit. Enjoy this!

Finally, it should be noted that the purpose of this book is admittedly narrow, given the larger context of Christian practice. Actually, there are numerous "habits of grace" that are essential to the full experience of God's grace in the life of the believer. Some of them are as follows: Bible meditation (Acts 20:32; Colossians 3:16), faith (Hebrews 4:2), prayer (Hebrews 4:16), fellowship with the saints (Ephesians 4:29), humility (James 4:6), generosity (2 Corinthians 9:8-14), obedience (Titus 2:11-12), forgiveness (Ephesians 4:32), worship (Ephesians 1:6), and evangelism (2 Corinthians 5:18-20). My purpose here is merely to spotlight the first of these practices and to provide a specific method by which you can meditate on the gospel in a meaningful way. While preaching the gospel to yourself will powerfully enrich your life in every area, the other habits listed above should also be practiced in order for your experience of the gospel to be truly complete.

Nonetheless, this book is based on the premise that all Christians should become expert in their knowledge and use of the gospel, not simply so they can share it faithfully with non-Christians, but also so they can speak it to themselves every day and experience its benefits. In fact, if Christians would do more preaching of the gospel to themselves, non-Christians might have less trouble comprehending its message, for they would see its truth and power exuding from believers in indisputable ways. This book is offered as a service to this end.

Milton Vincent

Holy Trinity,
continue to teach me
that Christ's righteousness satisfies justice
and evidences thy love;
help me to make use of it by faith
as the ground of my peace
and of thy favour and acceptance,
so that I may live always near the cross.

The Valley of Vision
"Election"

PART I

Reasons to Rehearse the Gospel Daily

"The gospel isn't one class among many that you'll attend during your life as a Christian – the gospel is the whole building that all the classes take place in! Rightly approached, all the topics you'll study and focus on as a believer will be offered to you 'within the walls' of the glorious gospel."

C.J. Mahaney, *The Cross Centered Life*, 75-76

The New Testament Model

The New Testament teaches that Christians ought to hear the gospel as much as non-Christians do. In fact, in the first chapter of Romans the Apostle Paul tells the believers in the church that he was anxious *"to preach the gospel to you who are at Rome."*[1] Of course, he was anxious to preach the gospel to the non-Christians at Rome, yet he specifically states that he was eager to preach it to the believers as well.

To the Corinthian Christians who had already believed and been saved by the gospel, Paul says, *"I make known to you the gospel, which you have believed...."*[2] He then restates the historical facts of the gospel before showing them how those gospel facts apply to their beliefs about the afterlife. This is actually Paul's approach to various other issues throughout the book of 1 Corinthians.

In most of Paul's letters to churches, sizeable portions of them are given over to rehearsing gospel truths. For example, Ephesians 1-3 is all gospel, Colossians 1-2 is gospel, and Romans 1-11 is gospel. The remainder of such books shows specifically how to bring those gospel truths to bear on life. Re-preaching the gospel and then showing how it applied to life was Paul's choice method for ministering to believers, thereby providing a divinely inspired pattern for me to follow when ministering to myself and to other believers.

---

[1] **Romans 1:15.** "So, for my part, I am eager to preach the gospel to [lit. "evangelize"] you also who are in Rome."

[2] **1 Corinthians 15.** "(1) Now I make known to you, brethren, the gospel which I preached to you, which also you received, in which also you stand, (2) by which also you are saved, if you hold fast the word which I preached to you, unless you believed in vain. (3) For I delivered to you as of first importance . . . that Christ died for our sins according to the Scriptures, (4) and that He was buried, and that He was raised on the third day according to the Scriptures."

My Daily Need

The gospel is so foolish[3] (according to my natural wisdom), so scandalous[4] (according to my conscience), and so incredible (according to my timid heart[5]), that it is a daily battle to believe the full scope of it as I should. There is simply no other way to compete with the forebodings of my conscience, the condemnings of my heart, and the lies of the world and the Devil[6] than to overwhelm such things with daily rehearsings of the gospel.

The Power of God

Outside of heaven, the power of God in its highest density is found inside the gospel. This must be so, for the Bible twice describes the gospel as *"the power of God."*[7] Nothing else in all of Scripture is ever described in this way, except for the Person of Jesus Christ.[8] Such a description indicates that the

---

[3] **1 Corinthians 1.** "(21) For since . . . the world through its wisdom did not come to know God, God was well-pleased through the foolishness of the message preached to save those who believe. . . . (23) . . . we preach Christ crucified, . . . to Gentiles foolishness."

[4] **1 Corinthians 1:23.** ". . . we preach Christ crucified, . . . a stumbling block [Gr. skandalon] . . . ."

[5] **1 John 3.** "(19) We will know . . . that we are of the truth, and will assure our hearts before Him (20) in whatever our heart condemns us . . . ."

[6] **2 Corinthians 4:4.** ". . . the god of this world has blinded the minds of the unbelieving so that they might not see the light of the gospel of the glory of Christ . . . ."

[7] **Romans 1:16.** "For I am not ashamed of the gospel, for it is the power of God to salvation to everyone who believes . . . ." **1 Corinthians 1:18.** "For the word of the cross is foolishness to those who are perishing, but to us who are being saved it is the power of God."

[8] **1 Corinthians 1:24.** ". . .Christ the power of God. . ."

gospel is not only powerful, but that it is the ultimate entity in which God's power resides and does its greatest work.

Indeed, God's power is seen in erupting volcanos, in the unimaginably hot boil of our massive sun, and in the lightning speed of a recently discovered star seen streaking through the heavens at 1.5 million miles per hour. Yet in Scripture such wonders are never labeled *"the power of God."* How powerful, then, must the gospel be that it would merit such a title! And how great is the salvation it could accomplish in my life, if I would only embrace it by faith[9] and give it a central place in my thoughts each day!

My Daily Protection

As long as I am inside the gospel, I experience all the protection I need from the powers of evil that rage against me. It is for this reason that the Bible tells me to *"take up"*[10] and *"put on"*[11] the whole armor of God; and the pieces of armor it tells me to put on are all merely synonyms for the gospel. Translated literally from the Greek, they are: *". . . the salvation . . . the justification . . . truth . . . the gospel of peace*

---

[9]**Hebrews 4:2.** "For indeed we have had good news preached to us, just as they also; but the word they heard did not profit them, because it was not united by faith in those who heard." **Ephesians 1.** "(18) I pray that the eyes of your heart may be enlightened, so that you will know . . . (19) . . . what is the surpassing greatness of His power toward us who believe."

[10]**Ephesians 6:13.** "Therefore, take up the full armor of God, so that you will be able to resist in the evil day . . . ."

[11]**Ephesians 6.** "(11) Put on the full armor of God, so that you will be able to stand firm against the schemes of the devil. (12) For our struggle is not against flesh and blood, but against the rulers, against the powers, against the world forces of this darkness, against the spiritual forces of wickedness in the heavenly places."

. . . the faith . . . [and the] . . . word of God."[12] What are all these expressions but various ways of describing the gospel? Therefore, if I wish to stand victorious in Jesus, I must do as the songwriter suggests and *"put on the gospel armor, each piece put on with prayer."*[13]

That God would tell me to *"take up"* and *"put on"* this gospel armor alerts me to the fact that I do not automatically come into each day protected by the gospel. In fact, these commands imply that I am vulnerable to defeat and injury unless I seize upon the gospel and arm myself with it from head to toe. And what better way is there to do this than to preach the gospel to myself and to make it the obsession of my heart throughout each day?

Transformed by Glory

The glory of God is the most powerful agent of transformation available to mankind. It is so powerful that it transforms those who merely gaze upon it. The Apostle Paul gives personal testimony concerning this stunning fact. *"But we all,"* he says, *"beholding as in a mirror the glory of the Lord, are being transformed into the same image from glory to glory."*[14] From Paul's testimony I learn that if I wish to become all that God wants me to be, I must behold His glory each day.

---

[12]**Ephesians 6.** "(14) Stand firm therefore, having girded your loins with truth, and having put on the breastplate of righteousness, (15) and having shod your feet with the preparation of the gospel of peace; (16) in addition to all, taking up the shield of faith with which you will be able to extinguish all the flaming arrows of the evil one. (17) And take the helmet of salvation, and the sword of the Spirit, which is the word of God."

[13]"Stand Up, Stand Up for Jesus," written by George Duffield, Jr., (1818-1888).

[14]**2 Corinthians 3:18.** "But we all, with unveiled face, beholding as in a mirror the glory of the Lord, are being transformed into the same image from glory to glory, just as from the Lord, the Spirit."

But where do I find God's glory to behold? Indeed, the glory of God is revealed throughout all of Creation,[15] but the Bible indicates that, outside of heaven, the glory of God in its thickest density dwells inside the gospel. It is for this reason that the gospel is described in Scripture as *"the gospel of the glory of Christ"* and *"the gospel of the glory of the blessed God."*[16] Consequently, as I habitually gaze upon the glory of the Lord revealed in the gospel, I can know that actual deposits of God's very glory are attaching themselves to my person and transforming me from one level of glory to another.[17] This transformation is deep and abiding, and unfadingly displays the glory of God to others.[18]

A Cure for Distrust

Every time I deliberately disobey a command of God, it is because I am in that moment doubtful as to God's true intentions in giving me that command. Does He really have my best interests at heart? Or is He withholding something from me that I would be better off having?[19] Such questions,

---

[15]**Psalm 19:1**. "The heavens are telling of the glory of God . . . ."
Isaiah 6:3. ". . . 'Holy, Holy, Holy, is the Lord of hosts, the whole earth is full of His glory.'"

[16]**2 Corinthians 4:4**. ". . . the light of the gospel of the glory of Christ..."
1 Timothy 1:11. ". . . the gospel of the glory of the blessed God . . . ." *(literal translation)*

[17]**2 Corinthians 3:18**. "But we all, with unveiled face, beholding as in a mirror the glory of the Lord, are being transformed into the same image from glory to glory, just as from the Lord, the Spirit."

[18]**2 Corinthians 3:13**. "and [we] are not like Moses, who used to put a veil over his face so that the sons of Israel would not look intently at the end of that which was fading away."

[19]**Genesis 3**. "(4) The serpent said, '. . . (5) . . . God knows that in the day you eat from it your eyes will be opened, and you will be like God, knowing good and evil.' (6) When the woman saw that the tree was good for food, and that it was a delight to the eyes, and that the tree was desirable to make one wise, she took from its fruit and ate. . ."

whether consciously asked or not, lie underneath every act of disobedience.

However, the gospel changes my view of God's commandments, in that it helps me to see the heart of the Person from whom those commandments come. When I begin my train of thought with the gospel, I realize that if God loved me enough to sacrifice His Son's life for me, then He must be guided by that same love when He speaks His commandments to me. Viewing God's commands and prohibitions in this light, I can see them for what they really are: friendly signposts from a heavenly Father who is seeking to love me through each directive, so that I might experience His very fullness forever.[20]

When controlling my thoughts as described above, the gospel cures me of my suspicion of God, thereby disposing me to walk more trustingly on the path of obedience to His commands.

Sufficiency in the Gospel

The gospel serves as the means by which God daily constructs me into what He wants me to be and also serves as the channel through which He gives me my inheritance every day of my Christian life.[21] Hence, it could be said that the gospel contains all that I need *"for life and godliness."*[22] It is

---

[20]**Deuteronomy 5:29**. "Oh that they had such a heart in them, that they would . . . keep all My commandments always, that it may be well with them and with their sons forever!"

[21]**Acts 20:32**. ". . . I commend you . . . to the message of His grace [the gospel], which is continually able to build you up and give you the inheritance among all those who are sanctified." *(literal translation)*

[22]**2 Peter 1:3**. ". . . His divine power has granted to us everything pertaining to life and godliness, through the true knowledge of Him who called us by His own glory and excellence."

for this reason that God tells me to be steadfastly entrenched in the gospel at all times and never to allow myself to be moved from there.[23] The mere fact that God tells me to stay inside the gospel at all times must mean that He intends to supply all of my needs as long as I am abiding in that place of luxury.[24]

Freedom from Sin's Power

As long as I am stricken with the guilt of my sins, I will be captive to them, and will often find myself re-committing the very sins about which I feel most guilty. The Devil is well aware of this fact; he knows that if he can keep me tormented by sin's guilt, he can dominate me with sin's power.

The gospel, however, slays sin at this root point and thereby nullifies sin's power over me. The forgiveness of God, made known to me through the gospel, liberates me from sin's power because it liberates me first from its guilt;[25] and preaching such forgiveness to myself is a practical way of putting the gospel into operation as a nullifier of sin's power in my life.

---

[23]**Colossians 1:23.** ". . . continue in the faith firmly established and stead-fast, and not moved away from the hope of the gospel . . . ."

[24]**Colossians 2.** "(8) See to it that no one takes you captive through phi-losophy and empty deception, according to the tradition of men, according to the elementary principles of the world, rather than according to Christ. (9) For in Him all the fullness of Deity dwells in bodily form, (10) and in Him you have been made complete . . . ." **2 Peter 1:3.** ". . . His divine power has granted to us everything pertaining to life and godliness, through the true knowledge of Him who called us by His own glory and excellence."

[25]**Romans 6:14.** "For sin shall not be master over you, for you are . . . under grace."

Resting in Christ's Righteousness

The gospel encourages me to rest in my righteous standing with God, a standing which Christ Himself has accomplished and always maintains for me.[26] I never have to do a moment's labor to gain or maintain my justified status before God![27] Freed from the burden of such a task, I now can put my energies into enjoying God, pursuing holiness, and ministering God's amazing grace to others.

The gospel also reminds me that my righteous standing with God always holds firm regardless of my performance, because my standing is based solely on the work of Jesus and not mine.[28] On my worst days of sin and failure, the gospel encourages me with God's unrelenting grace toward me.[29] On my best days of victory and usefulness, the gospel keeps me relating to God solely on the basis of Jesus' righteousness and not mine.

---

[26]**Romans 5.** "(1) Therefore, having been justified by faith, we have peace with God through our Lord Jesus Christ, (2) through whom also we have obtained our introduction by faith into this grace in which we stand; and we exult in hope of the glory of God." **1 John 2.** "(1) . . . And if anyone sins, we have an Advocate with the Father, Jesus Christ the righteous; (2) and He Himself is the propitiation for our sins . . . ."

[27]**Romans 4:5.** "But to the one who does not work, but believes in Him who justifies the ungodly, his faith is credited as righteousness," **Hebrews 4:3.** "For we who have believed enter that rest . . . ." **Matthew 11:28.** "Come to Me, all who are weary and heavy-laden, and I will give you rest."

[28]**Romans 5.** "(18) So then as through one transgression there resulted condemnation to all men, even so through one act of righteousness there resulted justification of life to all men. (19) . . . through the obedience of the One the many will be made righteous."

[29]**Romans 5.** "(20) . . . where sin increased, grace abounded all the more, (21) so that, as sin reigned in death, even so grace would reign through righteousness to eternal life through Jesus Christ our Lord. (6:1) What shall we say then? Are we to continue in sin so that grace might increase?" **1 John 2.** "(1) . . . And if anyone sins, we have an Advocate with the Father, Jesus Christ the righteous; (2) and He Himself is the propitiation for our sins . . . ."

Enslaved by Christ's Righteousness

The righteousness of God, credited to me through Christ, is not merely something I rest in, but it is also the premier saving reality by which God governs me. According to Romans 6, when I obeyed the gospel call I was both declared righteous and *"became a slave to righteousness"* at the same time.[30] Quite literally, the righteousness that God credited to me became my master on the day I was converted! And now I am daily called by God to surrender the members of my being as slaves to do whatever this righteousness dictates.[31]

That I would be called to present my members as slaves of this imputed righteousness implies that my justification has something to say to me by way of directing me how to live my life each day. What it directs me to do is to be holy; and what results from my obedience to its rule is sanctification, or holiness of life.[32] Hence, it could be said that 'sanctification' is merely the lifelong process wherein I joyfully surrender myself to God's imputed righteousness and then do whatever this righteousness directs me to do. Indeed, God has clothed me with His righteousness. Now He wants this righteousness to master me.

The more I exult in the reality of my justification in Christ, the more I position myself to experience the full

---

[30]**Romans 6.** "(17) But thanks be to God that . . . you became obedient from the heart to that form of teaching to which you were committed, (18) and having been freed from sin, you became slaves of righteousness." *(literal translation = "slaves of the righteousness")*

[31]**Romans 6:19**. ". . . For just as you presented your members as slaves to impurity and to lawlessness, resulting in further lawlessness, so now present your members as slaves to righteousness, resulting in sanctification."

[32]**Romans 6:19**. ". . . so now present your members as slaves to righteousness, resulting in sanctification."

governing force of its sanctifying power in my life. And the more sanctified I become, the more I experience the full breadth of eternal life that God has given to me in Christ.[33]

Loving My Brothers and Sisters

The more I experience the gospel, the more there develops within me a yearning affection for my fellow-Christians who are also participating in the glories of the gospel. This affection for them comes loaded with confidence in their continued spiritual growth and ultimate glorification, and it becomes my pleasure to express to them this loving confidence regarding the ongoing work of God in their lives.[34]

Additionally, with the gospel proving itself to be such a boon in my own life, I realize that the greatest gift I can give to my fellow-Christians is the gospel itself. Indeed, I love my fellow-Christians not simply because of the gospel, but I love them best when I am loving them with the gospel![35] And I do this not merely by speaking gospel words to them, but also by living before them and generously relating to them in a gospel manner. Imparting my life to them in this way,

---

[33]**Romans 6.** "(19) . . . so now present your members as slaves to righteousness, resulting in sanctification. . . . (22) But now having been freed from sin and enslaved to God, you derive your benefit, resulting in sanctification, and the outcome, eternal life."

[34]**Philippians 1.** "(3) I thank my God in all my remembrance of you, (4) always offering prayer with joy in my every prayer for you all, (5) in view of your participation in the gospel from the first day until now. (6) For I am confident of this very thing, that He who began a good work in you will perfect it until the day of Christ Jesus. (7) For it is only right for me to feel this way about you all, because I have you in my heart, since both in my imprisonment and in the defense and confirmation of the gospel, you all are partakers of grace with me."

[35]**1 Thessalonians 2:8.** "Having so fond an affection for you, we were well-pleased to impart to you not only the gospel of God but also our own lives, because you had become very dear to us."

I thereby contribute to their experience of the power, the Spirit, and the full assurance of the gospel.[36]

By preaching the gospel to myself each day, I nurture the bond that unites me with my brothers and sisters for whom Christ died, and I also keep myself well-versed in the raw materials with which I may actively love them in Christ.

My Inheritance in the Saints

The gospel is not just a message of reconciliation with God, but it also heralds the reconciliation of all believers to one another in Christ. Through the death of Christ, God has brought peace where there was once hostility, and He has broken down the racial, economic, and social barriers that once divided us outside of Christ.[37]

Also, when God saved us, He made us members of His household,[38] and He gave us as gifts to one another.[39] Each brother and sister is a portion of my gospel inheritance from

---

[36]**1 Thessalonians 1:5.** "For our gospel did not come to you in word only, but also in power, and in the Holy Spirit and in much assurance, as you know what kind of men we were among you for your sake." *(New King James Version)*

[37]**Ephesians 2.** "(14) For He Himself is our peace, who made both groups into one and broke down the barrier of the dividing wall, (15) by abolishing in His flesh the enmity . . . so that in Himself He might make the two into one new man, thus establishing peace, (16) and might reconcile them both in one body to God through the cross, by it having put to death the enmity." **Colossians 3:11.** "a renewal in which there is no distinction between Greek and Jew, circumcised and uncircumcised, barbarian, Scythian, slave and freeman, but Christ is all, and in all." **Galatians 3:28.** "There is neither Jew nor Greek, there is neither slave nor free man, there is neither male nor female; for you are all one in Christ Jesus." **Revelation 5:9.** "'. . . You [Jesus] were slain, and purchased for God with Your blood men from every tribe and tongue and people and nation.'"

[38]**Ephesians 2:19.** "So then you are no longer strangers and aliens, but you are fellow citizens with the saints, and are of God's household,"

[39]**Ephesians 1:18.** "I pray that the eyes of your heart may be enlightened, so that you will know . . . what are the riches of the glory of His inheritance in the saints,"

God, and I am a portion of their inheritance as well. We are significant players in each other's gospel narrative, and it is in relationship with one another that we experience the fullness of God in Christ.[40]

Hence, the more I comprehend the full scope of the gospel, the more I value the church for which Christ died,[41] the more I value the role that I play in the lives of my fellow-Christians, and the more I appreciate the role that they must be allowed to play in mine.

Stimulated to Love Others

When my mind is fixed on the gospel, I have ample stimulation to show God's love to other people. For I am always willing to show love to others when I am freshly mindful of the love that God has shown me.[42] Also, the gospel gives me the wherewithal to give forgiving grace to

---

[40]**Ephesians 3.** "(17) . . . you, being rooted and grounded in love, (18) may be able to comprehend with all the saints what is the breadth and length and height and depth, (19) and to know the love of Christ . . . , that you may be filled up to all the fullness of God." **2 Timothy 2:22.** ". . . pursue righteousness, faith, love and peace, with those who call on the Lord from a pure heart." **1 Peter 4:10.** "As each one has received a special gift, employ it in serving one another as good stewards of the manifold grace of God." **Ephesians 1.** "(22) . . . the church, (23) which is His body, the fullness of Him who fills all in all."

[41]**Ephesians 5:25.** ". . . Christ . . . loved the church and gave Himself up for her,"

[42]**Titus 3.** "(1) Remind them . . . (2) to malign no one, to be peaceable, gentle, showing every consideration for all men. (3) For we also once were foolish ourselves, disobedient, deceived, enslaved to various lusts and pleasures, spending our life in malice and envy, hateful, hating one another. (4) But when the kindness of God our Savior and His love for mankind appeared, (5) He saved us, not on the basis of deeds which we have done in righteousness, but according to His mercy, by the washing of regeneration and renewing by the Holy Spirit, (6) whom He poured out upon us richly through Jesus Christ our Savior, (7) so that being justified by His grace we would be made heirs according to the hope of eternal life. (8) This is a trustworthy statement; and concerning these things I want you to speak confidently, so that those who have believed God will be careful to engage in good deeds. These things are good and profitable for men."

24

those who have wronged me, for it reminds me daily of the forgiving grace that God is showing me.[43]

Doing good and showing love to those who have wronged me is always the opposite of what my sinful flesh wants me to do. Nonetheless, when I remind myself of my sins against God and of His forgiving and generous grace toward me, I give the gospel an opportunity to reshape my perspective and to put me in a frame of mind wherein I actually desire to give this same grace to those who have wronged me.

A Heart for the Lost

The more I rehearse and exult in gospel truths, the more there develops within me a corresponding burden for non-Christians to enter into such blessings. This is also what seems to happen to the Apostle Paul while writing the book of Romans.

In Romans 5 Paul exults in his righteous standing before God.[44] In chapter 6 he speaks of the freedom from sin which Christ has accomplished in the lives of believers,[45] a freedom which Paul later confesses had not yet become fully realized in

---

[43]**Ephesians 4:32.** "Be kind to one another, tender-hearted, forgiving each other, just as God in Christ also has forgiven you." **Colossians 3.** "(12) So, as those who have been chosen of God, holy and beloved, put on a heart of compassion, kindness, humility, gentleness and patience; (13) bearing with one another, and forgiving each other, whoever has a complaint against anyone; just as the Lord forgave you, so also should you."

[44]**Romans 5.** "(1) Therefore, having been justified by faith, we have peace with God through our Lord Jesus Christ, . . . (2) . . . and we exult . . . . (3) . . . we . . . exult . . . . (11) . . . we exult . . . ."

[45]**Romans 6.** "(1) What shall we say then? Are we to continue in sin so that grace may increase? (2) May it never be! How shall we who died to sin still live in it?" **Romans 6:6.** "knowing this, that our old self was crucified with Him, in order that our body of sin might be done away with, so that we would no longer be slaves to sin;"

his own daily practice (chapter 7).[46] Nonetheless, coming into chapter 8, he recounts the fact that there is no condemnation for those who are in Christ Jesus.[47] With increasing flourish, he rehearses numerous gospel themes throughout the length of chapter 8, and he climaxes the chapter with a triumphant exclamation regarding the endless love of God which enables Christians to conquer overwhelmingly in all things.[48]

What effect do such gospel meditations have upon Paul? What emotions do they produce in him besides the obvious joy he feels while reciting them? Paul bares his soul at the very beginning of chapter 9: *"I have great sorrow,"* he says, *"and unceasing grief in my heart. For I could wish that I myself were accursed, separated from Christ, for the sake of my brethren, my kinsmen according to the flesh."*[49]

Coming down from the heights of gospel meditation, Paul's heart is devastated by a burden for his fellow-Jews to experience the saving power of the gospel. His burden existed long before he started writing, but it is undoubtedly intensified by his rehearsal of gospel truths in Romans 5-8, a rehearsal which inevitably leads his thoughts toward the plight of those outside of Christ.

---

[46]**Romans 7:19.** "For the good that I want, I do not do, but I practice the very evil that I do not want."

[47]**Romans 8:1.** "Therefore there is now no condemnation for those who are in Christ Jesus."

[48]**Romans 8.** "(35) Who will separate us from the love of Christ? Will tribulation, or distress, or persecution, or famine, or nakedness, or peril, or sword? . . . (37) But in all these things we overwhelmingly conquer through Him who loved us. (38) For I am convinced that neither death, nor life, nor angels, nor principalities, nor things present, nor things to come, nor powers, (39) nor height, nor depth, nor any other created thing, will be able to separate us from the love of God, which is in Christ Jesus our Lord."

[49]**Romans 9.** "(1) I am telling the truth in Christ, . . . (2) that I have great sorrow and unceasing grief in my heart. (3) For I could wish that I myself were accursed, separated from Christ for the sake of my brethren, my kinsmen according to the flesh, (4) who are Israelites . . . ."

Hence, if I wish to have a 'Romans 9' kind of burden for non-Christians, I should become practiced at celebrating the gospel as Paul does in Romans 5-8. Over time, my joy in the gospel will become increasingly tinged with grief, and this grief-stained joy will lend a God-inspired passion to my ministry of evangelizing the lost.

Cultivating Humility

According to Scripture, God deliberately designed the gospel in such a way so as to strip me of pride and leave me without any grounds for boasting in myself whatsoever.[50] This is actually a wonderful mercy from God, for pride is at the root of all my sin. Pride produced the first sin in the Garden,[51] and pride always precedes every sinful stumbling in my life.[52] Therefore, if I am to experience deliverance from sin, I must be delivered from the pride that produces it. Thankfully, the gospel is engineered to accomplish this deliverance.

Preaching the gospel to myself each day mounts a powerful assault against my pride and serves to establish humility in its place. Nothing suffocates my pride more than

---

[50]**Ephesians 2.** "(8) For by grace you have been saved through faith; and that not of yourselves, it is the gift of God; (9) not as a result of works, so that no one may boast." **1 Corinthians 1.** "(27) but God has chosen the foolish things of the world to shame the wise, and God has chosen the weak things of the world to shame the things which are strong, (28) and the base things of the world and the despised God has chosen, the things that are not, so that He might nullify the things that are, (29) so that no man may boast before God."

[51]**Genesis 3.** "(4) The serpent said, '. . . (5) . . . God knows that in the day you eat from it your eyes will be opened, and you will be like God, knowing good and evil.' (6) When the woman saw that the tree . . . was desirable to make one wise, she took from its fruit and ate . . . .'"

[52]**Proverbs 16:18.** "Pride goes before destruction, a haughty spirit before stumbling."

daily reminders regarding the glory of my God, the gravity of my sins, and the crucifixion of God's own Son in my place. Also, the gracious love of God, lavished on me because of Christ's death, is always humbling to remember, especially when viewed against the backdrop of the Hell I deserve.

Pride wilts in the atmosphere of the gospel; and the more pride is mortified within me, the less frequent are my moments of sinful contention with God and with others.[53] Conversely, humility grows lushly in the atmosphere of the gospel, and the more humility flourishes within me, the more I experience God's grace[54] along with the strengthening His grace provides.[55] Additionally, such humility intensifies my passion for God and causes my heart increasingly to thrill whenever He is praised.[56]

Obedience Borne of Love

To love God with all my heart, soul, mind, and strength is the greatest commandment in the Law.[57] If I could simply fulfill this one commandment, I would gladly fulfill all others as a natural matter of course.

---

[53]**Proverbs 13:10**. "By pride comes nothing but strife . . . ." *(New King James Version)*

[54]**James 4:6**. ". . . God is opposed to the proud, but gives grace to the humble."

[55]**Hebrews 13:9**. " . . . it is good for the heart to be strengthened by grace..."

[56]**Psalm 34:2**. "My soul shall make its boast in the Lord; the humble shall hear it and rejoice."

[57]**Mark 12**. "(28) . . . 'What commandment is the foremost of all?' . . . . (30) '. . . you shall love the Lord your God with all your heart, and with all your soul, and with all your mind, and with all your strength.'"

So how can I come to love God with all of my being?[58] The Bible teaches that genuine love in my heart for God is generated by an awareness of His love for me,[59] and nowhere is the love of God more clearly revealed than in the gospel.[60]

Therefore, preaching the gospel to myself is a great way to keep God's amazing love before my eyes, so that I might experience its power to produce in me a passionate love for Him in return. Captured by His love in this way, my smitten heart increasingly burns to do His will and feasts itself on doing so.[61]

Liberation from Self-Love

Compared to greater endeavors, self-love is mundane and tiresome. Consequently, the more thoroughly I can be done with such tedium, the freer my soul will be to soar at its God-intended heights.

One of the leading causes of my natural tendency to self-love is fear. I fear that if I do not love myself there would be no one left to love me quite so well as I do. An even more significant cause of self-love is a lack of persuasion that there

---

[58]**1 John 5:3**. "For this is the love of God, that we keep His commandments; and His commandments are not burdensome."

[59]**1 John 4:19**. "We love, because He first loved us."

[60]**Romans 5**. "(7) For one will hardly die for a righteous man; though perhaps for the good man someone would dare even to die. (8) But God demonstrates His own love toward us, in that while we were yet sinners, Christ died for us." **John 15:13**. "Greater love has no one than this, that one lay down his life for his friends." **Ephesians 2**. "(4) But God, being rich in mercy, because of His great love with which He loved us, (5) even when we were dead in our transgressions, made us alive together with Christ . . . ,"

[61]**John 14:31**. ". . . so that the world may know that I love the Father, I do exactly as the Father commanded Me..." **John 4:34**. "Jesus said to them, 'My food is to do the will of Him who sent Me and to accomplish His work.'" **Psalm 40:8**. "I delight to do Your will, O my God; Your Law is within my heart."

is someone out there who is worthy to be loved more than I. Arrogance lies underneath both of these causes: I love myself supremely because I am the most worthy person I know to be loved and also because I think I can do a better job at it than anyone else. Such arrogance makes me dangerous,[62] yet it is deeply ingrained in my sinful flesh.

Thankfully, the gospel frees me from the shackles of self-love by addressing both of these causes. First, the gospel assures me that the love of God is infinitely superior to any love that I could ever give to myself. *"Greater love has no one than this,"* says Jesus while speaking of His love.[63] And the deeper I go into the gospel, the more I experience the truth of His claim and thereby know how far His love for me surpasses even my own.[64] His astonishing love for me renders self-absorption moot and frees me up to move on to causes and interests far greater than myself.[65]

Second, the gospel reveals to me the breathtaking glory and loveliness of God,[66] and in so doing, it lures my heart away from love of self and leaves me enthralled by Him instead. The more I behold God's glory in the gospel, the more lovely He appears to me. And the more lovely He

---

[62]**2 Timothy 3**. "(1) But know this, that in the last days perilous times will come: (2) For men will be lovers of themselves . . ." *(New King James Version)*

[63]**John 15:13**. "Greater love has no one than this, that one lay down his life for his friends."

[64]**Romans 8:32**. "He who did not spare His own Son, but delivered Him over for us all, how will He not also with Him freely give us all things?"

[65]**2 Corinthians 5**. "(14) For the love of Christ controls us, having concluded this, that one died for all, therefore all died; (15) and He died for all, so that they who live might no longer live for themselves, but for Him who died and rose again on their behalf."

[66]**2 Corinthians 4:4**. ". . . the gospel of the glory of Christ . . . ." **1 Timothy 1:11**. ". . . the gospel of the glory of the blessed God . . . ." *(literal translation)*

appears, the more self fades into the background like a former love interest who can no longer compete for my affections.

Preaching the gospel to myself every day reminds me of God's astounding love for me and also of His infinite worthiness to be loved by me above all else. These reminders deliver a one-two punch to my innate self-absorption and leave me increasingly absorbed with Christ[67] and with God's ultimate plan to gather together all heavenly and earthly things in Him.[68]

Perspective in Trials

More than anything else I could ever do, the gospel enables me to embrace my tribulations and thereby position myself to gain full benefit from them. For the gospel is the one great permanent circumstance in which I live and move; and every hardship in my life is allowed by God only because it serves His gospel purposes in me. When I view my circumstances in this light, I realize that the gospel is not just one piece of good news that fits into my life somewhere among all the bad. I realize instead that the gospel makes genuinely good news out of every other aspect of my life,

---

[67]**Philippians 3.** "(7) But whatever things were gain to me, those things I have counted as loss for the sake of Christ. (8) More than that, I count all things to be loss in view of the surpassing value of knowing Christ Jesus my Lord, for whom I have suffered the loss of all things, and count them but rubbish so that I may gain Christ,"

[68]**Ephesians 1.** "(9) He made known to us the mystery of His will, according to His kind intention which He purposed in Him (10) with a view to an administration suitable to the fullness of the times, that is, the summing up of all things in Christ, things in the heavens and things on the earth. . ." **1 Corinthians 15:28.** "When all things are subjected to Him, then the Son Himself also will be subjected to the One who subjected all things to Him, so that God may be all in all."

including my severest trials.[69] The good news about my trials is that God is forcing them to bow to His gospel purposes and do good unto me by improving my character and making me more conformed to the image of Christ.[70]

Preaching the gospel to myself each day provides a lens through which I can view my trials in this way and see the true cause for rejoicing that exists in them. I can then embrace trials as friends and allow them to do God's good work in me.

Exposed by the Cross, Part I

It was while rehearsing gospel truths in Romans 5-8 that the Apostle Paul was moved to speak of his struggle with sin and exclaim, "*O wretched man that I am!*"[71] While reviewing

---

[69]**Romans 5.** "(1) . . . having been justified by faith, we have peace with God through our Lord Jesus Christ, (2) . . . and we exult in hope of the glory of God. (3) And not only this, but we also exult in our tribulations, knowing that tribulation brings about perseverance; (4) and perseverance, proven character; and proven character, hope; (5) and hope does not disappoint, because the love of God has been poured out within our hearts through the Holy Spirit who was given to us."

[70]**Romans 8**. "(28) And we know that God causes all things to work together for good to those who love God, to those who are called according to His purpose. (29) For those whom He foreknew, He also predestined to become conformed to the image of His Son . . . ." **James 1.** "(2) Consider it all joy, my brethren, when you encounter various trials, (3) knowing that the testing of your faith produces endurance. (4) And let endurance have its perfect result, so that you may be perfect and complete, lacking in nothing." **2 Corinthians 12.** "(7) . . . there was given me a thorn in the flesh, a messenger of Satan to torment me – to keep me from exalting myself! (8) Concerning this I implored the Lord three times that it might leave me. (9) And He has said to me, 'My grace is sufficient for you, for power is perfected in weakness.' Most gladly, therefore, I will rather boast about my weaknesses, so that the power of Christ may dwell in me. (10) Therefore I am well content with weaknesses, with insults, with distresses, with persecutions, with difficulties, for Christ's sake; for when I am weak, then I am strong."

[71]**Romans 7.** "(19) For the good that I want, I do not do, but I practice the very evil that I do not want. . . . (23) . . . I see a different law in the members of my body, waging war against the law of my mind and making me a prisoner of the law of sin which is in my members. (24) Wretched man that I am! Who will set me free from the body of this death?"

God's abundant saving grace on another occasion, Paul was prompted to confess that he was the *"the foremost"* sinner of all.[72]

Likewise, the deeper I go into the gospel, the more I comprehend and confess aloud the depth of my sinfulness. A gruesome death like the one that Christ endured for me would only be required for one who is exceedingly sinful and unable to appease a holy God. Consequently, whenever I consider the necessity and manner of His death, along with the love and selflessness behind it, I am laid bare and utterly exposed[73] for the sinner I am.

Such an awareness of my sinfulness does not drag me down, but actually serves to lift me up by magnifying my appreciation of God's forgiving grace in my life. And the more I appreciate the magnitude of God's forgiveness of my sins, the more I love Him and delight to show Him love through heart-felt expressions of worship.[74]

---

[72]**1 Timothy 1:15.** "It is a trustworthy statement, deserving full acceptance, that Christ Jesus came into the world to save sinners, among whom I am foremost of all."

[73]**Hebrews 4:13.** ". . . all things are open and laid bare to the eyes of Him with whom we have to do."

[74]**Luke 7.** "(37) And there was a woman in the city who was a sinner; and when she learned that [Jesus] was reclining at the table in the Pharisee's house, she brought an alabaster vial of perfume, (38) and standing behind Him at His feet, weeping, she began to wet His feet with her tears, and kept wiping them with the hair of her head, and kissing His feet and anointing them with the perfume. . . . (40) And Jesus answered him, 'Simon, I have something to say to you.' And he replied, 'Say it, Teacher.' (41) 'A moneylender had two debtors: one owed five hundred denarii, and the other fifty. (42) When they were unable to repay, he graciously forgave them both. So which of them will love him more?' (43) Simon answered and said, 'I suppose the one whom he forgave more.' And He said to him, 'You have judged correctly.' (44) Turning toward the woman, He said to Simon, 'Do you see this woman? . . . she has wet My feet with her tears and wiped them with her hair. (45) . . . since the time I came in, [she] has not ceased to kiss My feet. (46) . . . she anointed My feet with perfume. (47) For this reason I say to you, her sins, which are many, have been forgiven, for she loved much; but he who is forgiven little, loves little.'"

Exposed by the Cross, Part II

The Cross also exposes me before the eyes of other people, informing them of the depth of my depravity. If I wanted others to think highly of me, I would conceal the fact that a shameful slaughter of the perfect Son of God was required that I might be saved. But when I stand at the foot of the Cross and am seen by others under the light of that Cross, I am left uncomfortably exposed before their eyes. Indeed, the most humiliating gossip that could ever be whispered about me is blared from Golgotha's hill;[75] and my self-righteous reputation is left in ruins in the wake of its revelations. With the worst facts about me thus exposed to the view of others, I find myself feeling that I truly have nothing left to hide.

Thankfully, the more exposed I see that I am by the Cross, the more I find myself opening up to others about ongoing issues of sin in my life. (Why would anyone be shocked to hear of my struggles with past and present sin when the Cross already told them I am a desperately sinful person?) And the more open I am in confessing my sins to fellow-Christians, the more I enjoy the healing of the Lord in response to their grace-filled counsel and prayers.[76] Experiencing richer levels of Christ's love in companionship with such saints,[77] I give

---

[75]Golgotha was the place where Jesus was crucified. **John 19.**"(17) ...and He went out, bearing His own cross, to the place called the Place of a Skull, which is called in Hebrew, Golgotha. (18) There they crucified Him . . . . "

[76]**James 5:16.** "Therefore, confess your sins to one another, and pray for one another so that you may be healed. . . . ."

[77]**Ephesians 3.** "(14) For this reason I bow my knees before the Father, . . . (17) . . . that you, being rooted and grounded in love, (18) may be able to comprehend with all the saints what is the breadth and length and height and depth, (19) and to know the love of Christ . . . ."

thanks for the gospel's role in forcing my hand toward self-disclosure and the freedom that follows.[78]

Chosen for Prayer

When God chose me in Christ before the foundation of the world, He did not merely choose me to be *"holy and blameless"*; He chose me also to be *"before Him in love."*[79] To be sure, I am always in God's presence on earth, and in heaven I will be in His presence more fully than ever. But it could also be said that in this life I am especially *"before Him in love"* when I come *"before Him"* in prayer and worship.[80]

Therefore, I can infer that prayer is not simply something I am allowed to do as a Christian; prayer is actually one of the great purposes for which God chose to save me. Christ Himself confirms this fact when He makes the following statement to His disciples: *"I chose you . . . that whatever you ask of the Father in My name He may give to you."*[81] As a chosen one of God, I was saved to pray; and whenever I come into God's presence to behold Him, worship Him, or make request of Him, I am arriving at the pinnacle of God's saving purposes for me.

---

[78]**Ecclesiastes 4**. "(9) Two are better than one . . . . (10) For if either of them falls, the one will lift up his companion. But woe to the one who falls when there is not another to lift him up. . . . (12) And if one can overpower him who is alone, two can resist him. A cord of three strands is not quickly torn apart."

[79]**Ephesians 1:4**. ". . . He chose us in Him before the foundation of the world, that we should be holy and without blame before Him in love," *(NKJV)*

[80]**Psalm 100:2**. "Serve the LORD with gladness; Come before Him with joyful singing." **Psalm 68:4**. "Sing to God, sing praises to His name . . . and exult before Him." **1 John 5:14**. "This is the confidence which we have before Him, that, if we ask anything according to His will, He hears us."

[81]**John 15:16**. "You did not choose Me but I chose you, and appointed you that you would go and bear fruit, and that your fruit would remain, so that whatever you ask of the Father in My name He may give to you."

God is radically committed to my life of prayer. He shed the blood of His Son so that I might be cleansed and rendered fit[82] to stand before Him in love. He also permitted the brutal rending of His Son so that I might now have a way into the Holy Place through the torn flesh of Jesus.[83] *"Draw near,"*[84] He says in Hebrews 4; *"draw near,"* He says in Hebrews 10;[85] *"pray without ceasing,"*[86] He urges elsewhere. How can I not feel the infinite sincerity of these invitations, especially when considering the painful lengths that God endured so that I might enter His presence in prayer?

Indeed, the gospel itself serves as the sweetest of invitations to pray; and preaching it to myself each day nurtures within me a mighty impulse to come *"before [God] in love"* and do the praying that I was elected to do.

Saved for Good Works

Through the gospel I learn not only of the saving works of God on my behalf, but I also learn that one of God's key purposes in doing these works is to put me to work myself.

The Bible tells me that when Christ redeemed me, He

---

[82]**Ephesians 1:7.** "In Him we have redemption through His blood, the forgiveness of our trespasses." **Romans 5:9.** "[we have] been justified by His blood."

[83]**Hebrews 10.** "(19) . . . we have confidence to enter the holy place by the blood of Jesus, (20) by a new and living way which He inaugurated for us through the veil, that is, His flesh . . ."

[84]**Hebrews 4:16.** "Therefore let us draw near with confidence to the throne of grace, so that we may receive mercy and find grace to help in time of need."

[85]**Hebrews 10.** "(19) Therefore, brethren, since we have confidence to enter the holy place by the blood of Jesus, (20) by a new and living way which He inaugurated for us through the veil, that is, His flesh, . . . (22) let us draw near with a sincere heart in full assurance of faith . . . ."

[86]**1 Thessalonians 5:17.** "Pray without ceasing;"

did so in order that I might now be *"zealous for good works."*[87] When God *"works"* in me day by day, He does so in order to produce in me the desire and the power to *"work for His good pleasure."*[88] Indeed, though I am saved by grace and not by works, I am God's *"workmanship, created in Christ Jesus <u>for good works</u>, which God prepared beforehand so that [I] would walk in them."*[89]

Being naturally lazy, I do not normally thrill at the prospect of work; but the more I embrace the saving work of God on my behalf, the more I find myself embracing the works for which God saved me. And as I am *"working hard"* at doing these works for the good of others, I experience the truth of Jesus' words: *"It is more blessed to give than to receive."*[90] I also find myself saying with Christ, *"My food is to do the will of Him who sent me and to accomplish His work."*[91] Indeed, gospel-motivated works do for the soul what food does for the body. They bring refreshment, enjoyment, blessing, and strengthening to the doer of the deeds, even more so than to the receiver. Hence, the fact that God has prepared such works for me to do becomes a part of what makes the gospel such great news to me.

---

[87]**Titus 2:14.** "who gave Himself for us to redeem us from every lawless deed, and to purify for Himself a people for His own possession, zealous for good deeds."

[88]**Philippians 2.** "(12) So then, my beloved, just as you have always obeyed, . . . work out your salvation with fear and trembling; (13) for it is God who is at work in you, both to will and to work for His good pleasure."

[89]**Ephesians 2:10.** "For we are His workmanship, created in Christ Jesus for good works, which God prepared beforehand so that we would walk in them."

[90]**Acts 20.** "(34) You yourselves know that these hands ministered to my own needs and to the men who were with me. (35) In everything I showed you that by working hard in this manner you must help the weak and remember the words of the Lord Jesus, that He Himself said, 'It is more blessed to give than to receive.'"

[91]**John 4.** "(32) But He said to them, 'I have food to eat that you do not know about.' (33) So the disciples were saying to one another, 'No one brought Him anything to eat, did he?' (34) Jesus said to them, 'My food is to do the will of Him who sent Me and to accomplish His work.'"

Preaching the gospel to myself each day not only reminds me of the love of God for me, but it also reminds me of the love of God for the works that He has saved me to perform. When I see the Cross, I see the premium that God places on the works that He has prepared for me. How valuable all of these works must be if Christ would die so that I might now perform them! And how precious are those for whom these works are done if Christ would die that they might be served!

A Heart for the Poor

Like nothing else could ever do, the gospel instills in me a heart for the downcast, the poverty-stricken, and those in need of physical mercies, especially when such persons are of the household of faith.[92]

When I see persons who are materially poor, I instantly feel a kinship with them, for they are physically what I was spiritually when my heart was closed to Christ.[93] Perhaps some of them are in their condition because of sin, but so was I. Perhaps they are unkind when I try to help them; but I, too, have been spiteful to God when He has sought to help me. Perhaps they are thankless and even abuse the kindness I show them, but how many times have I been thankless and used what God has given me to serve selfish ends?

Perhaps a poverty-stricken person will be blessed and changed as a result of some kindness I show him. If so, God

---

[92]**Galatians 6:10.** "So then, while we have opportunity, let us do good to all people, and especially to those who are of the household of the faith."

[93]**Revelation 3.** "'(17) . . . you are wretched and miserable and poor and blind and naked . . . . (20) Behold, I stand at the door and knock; if anyone hears My voice and opens the door, I will come in to him and will dine with him, and he with Me.'"

be praised for His grace through me. But if the person walks away unchanged by my kindness, then I still rejoice over the opportunity to love as God loves.[94] Perhaps the person will repent in time; but for now, my heart is chastened and made wiser by the tangible depiction of what I myself have done to God on numerous occasions.

The gospel reminds me daily of the spiritual poverty into which I was born[95] and also of the staggering generosity of Christ towards me.[96] Such reminders instill in me both a felt connection to the poor and a desire to show them the same generosity that has been lavished on me.[97] When ministering to the poor with these motivations, I not only preach the gospel to them through word and deed, but I reenact the gospel to my own benefit as well.

All Things Crucified, Part I

The gospel is not simply the story of *"Christ, and Him crucified"*[98]; it is also the story of my own crucifixion. For the

---

[94]**Matthew 5**. "(44) But I say to you, love your enemies . . . (45) so that you may be sons of your Father who is in heaven; for He causes His sun to rise on the evil and the good, and sends rain on the righteous and the unrighteous." **Romans 2:4**. "Or do you think lightly of the riches of His kindness and tolerance and patience, not knowing that the kindness of God leads you to repentance?"

[95]**Psalm 51:5**. "Behold, I was brought forth in iniquity, and in sin my mother conceived me."

[96]**2 Corinthians 8**. "(7) . . . see that you abound in this gracious work [of giving] . . . . (9) For you know the grace of our Lord Jesus Christ, that though He was rich, yet for your sake He became poor, so that you through His poverty might become rich." **Romans 8:32**. "He who did not spare His own Son, but delivered Him over for us all, how will He not also with Him freely give us all things?"

[97]**Ephesians 1**. "(7) . . . the riches of His grace (8) which He lavished on us. . . ."

[98]**1 Corinthians 2:2**. "For I determined to know nothing among you except Jesus Christ, and Him crucified."

Bible tells me that I, too, was crucified on Christ's cross.[99] My old self was slain there,[100] and my love affair with the world was crucified there too.[101] The cross is also the place where I crucify my flesh and all its sinful desires.[102] Truly, Christ's death and my death are so intertwined as to be inseparable.

God is committed to my dying every day, and He calls me to that same commitment.[103] He insists that every hour be my dying hour, and He wants my death on the cross to be as central to my own life story as is Christ's death to the gospel story. *"Let this same attitude be in you,"* He says, *"which was also in Christ Jesus . . . who became obedient unto death, even death on a cross."*[104]

Crucifixion hurts. In fact, its heart-wrenching brutality can numb the senses. It is a gasping and bloody affair, and there is nothing nice, pretty, or easy about it. It is not merely death, but excruciating death.

Nevertheless, I must set my face like a flint[105] toward the cross and embrace this crucifixion in everything I do.

---

[99]**Galatians 2:20.** "I have been crucified with Christ . . . ."

[100]**Romans 6:6.** "knowing this, that our old self was crucified with Him, in order that our body of sin might be done away with, so that we would no longer be slaves to sin;"

[101]**Galatians 6:14.** "But may it never be that I would boast, except in the cross of our Lord Jesus Christ, through which the world has been crucified to me, and I to the world."

[102]**Galatians 5:24.** "Now those who belong to Christ Jesus have crucified the flesh with its passions and desires."

[103]**Luke 9:23.** "And He was saying to them all, 'If anyone wishes to come after Me, he must deny himself, and take up his cross daily and follow Me.'"

[104]**Philippians 2.** "(5) Have this attitude in yourselves which was also in Christ Jesus, (6) who . . . (7) . . . emptied Himself, taking the form of a bond-servant, and being made in the likeness of men. (8) Being found in appearance as a man, He humbled Himself by becoming obedient to the point of death, even death on a cross."

[105]**Isaiah 50.** "(6) I gave My back to those who strike Me, and My cheeks to those who pluck out the beard; I did not cover My face from humiliation and spitting. (7) For the Lord God helps Me, therefore I am not disgraced; . . . I have set My face like flint, and I know that I shall not be ashamed."

I should expect every day to encounter circumstantial evidence of God's commitment to my dying; and I must seize upon every God-given opportunity to be conformed more fully to Christ's death, no matter the pain involved.

When my flesh yearns for some prohibited thing, I must die. When called to do something I don't want to do, I must die. When I wish to be selfish and serve no one, I must die. When shattered by hardships that I despise, I must die. When wanting to cling to wrongs done against me, I must die. When enticed by allurements of the world, I must die. When wishing to keep besetting sins secret, I must die. When wants that are borderline needs are left unmet, I must die. When dreams that are good seem shoved aside, I must die.

"Not My will, but Yours be done," Christ trustingly prayed on the eve of His crucifixion;[106] and preaching His story to myself each day puts me in a frame of mind to trust God and embrace the cross of my own dying also.[107]

All Things Crucified, Part II

Thankfully, the gospel teaches me that dying is not an end, but a beginning. For after Christ took up His cross

---

[106]**Luke 22:42.** ". . . 'Father, if You are willing, remove this cup from Me; yet not My will, but Yours be done." **1 Peter 2:23.** ". . . He . . . kept entrusting Himself to Him who judges righteously;'"

[107]**1 Peter 2.** "(21) For you have been called for this purpose, since Christ also suffered for you, leaving you an example for you to follow in His steps, (22) who committed no sin, nor was any deceit in His mouth; (23) and while being reviled, He did not revile in return; while suffering, He uttered no threats, but kept entrusting Himself to Him who judges righteously; (24) and He Himself bore our sins in His body on the cross, so that we might die to sin and live to righteousness . . . ." **1 Corinthians 15:31.** ". . . I die daily." **Romans 8:36.** ". . . we are being put to death all day long . . . ."

and died, God raised Him from the dead,[108] exalted Him to the highest heaven,[109] and drew Him into His bosom.[110] These facts surrounding Christ's resurrection stand as proof positive that God will not leave me for dead, but will raise me similarly, if I would only allow myself to die. Indeed, on the other side of each layer of dying lie experiences of a life with God that are far richer, far higher, and far more intimate than anything I would have otherwise known.[111]

In God's economy, death is the way to life. *"Whoever wishes to save his life will lose it,"* Jesus says, *"but whoever loses His life for My sake, he shall find it."*[112] Indeed, the more conformable I am made to the death of Christ, the more I experience freedom from sin[113] and taste the power of the resurrection of Jesus Himself.[114] The path to such power is paved with many dyings, and each stage of resurrection is achieved with each incident of dying to myself and reckoning myself dead to sin.[115]

---

[108]**Ephesians 1:20.** ". . . He raised Him from the dead . . ."

[109]**Philippians 2.** "(8) . . . He humbled Himself by becoming obedient to the point of death, even death on a cross. (9) For this reason also, God highly exalted Him, and bestowed on Him the name which is above every name,"

[110]**John 1:18.** "No one has seen God at any time; the only begotten God who is *[present tense]* in the bosom of the Father, He has explained Him."

[111]**Romans 6:4.** "Therefore we have been buried with Him through baptism into death, so that as Christ was raised from the dead through the glory of the Father, so we too might walk in newness of life."

[112]**Luke 9:24.** "For whoever wishes to save his life will lose it, but whoever loses his life for My sake, he is the one who will save it."

[113]**Romans 6.** "(6) knowing this, that our old self was crucified with Him, in order that our body of sin might be done away with, so that we would no longer be slaves to sin; (7) for he who has died is freed from sin."

[114]**Philippians 3.** "(8) . . . I count all things to be loss in view of the surpassing value of knowing Christ Jesus my Lord, for whom I have suffered the loss of all things, and count them but rubbish so that I may gain Christ . . . (10) that I may know Him and the power of His resurrection and the fellowship of His sufferings, being conformed to His death;"

[115]**Romans 6:11.** "Even so consider yourselves to be dead to sin, but alive to God in Christ Jesus."

The more I contemplate the gospel, the more I understand that this *"word of the cross"*[116] stands as a blueprint for my own life story. The death that Christ died is the death to which I also am called, and the death to which I am called is my entry point to union with Christ and life at its fullest.[117] So, come what may, I'll let no one take this death from me!

Hope of Heaven

The more I experience the riches of Christ in the gospel, the more there develops within me a yearning to be with Christ in heaven where I will experience His grace in unhindered fullness.[118] The reason for this yearning is simple: however great may be the present blessings of salvation, they are but the *"first fruits of the Spirit,"* the first installments of an unimaginably great harvest of glory which I will reap forever in heaven.[119]

The Apostle Paul could not rehearse gospel blessings in Romans 5-8 without being reminded of his anxious longing for the future glories awaiting believers in heaven.[120] Likewise, the Apostle John could not speak of his and his readers' status as children of God without also relishing the

---

[116]**1 Corinthians 1:18**. "For the word of the cross is foolishness to those who are perishing, but to us who are being saved it is the power of God."

[117]**Romans 6:5**. "For if we have become united with Him in the likeness of His death, certainly we shall also be in the likeness of His resurrection . . . ."

[118]**Philippians 1:23**. "But I . . . [have] the desire to depart and be with Christ, for that is very much better;" **1 Peter 1:13**. ". . . fix your hope completely on the grace to be brought to you at the revelation of Jesus Christ."

[119]**Romans 8:23**. ". . . we ourselves, having the first fruits of the Spirit . . . ."

[120]**Romans 8**. "(18) For I consider that the sufferings of this present time are not worthy to be compared with the glory that is to be revealed to us. (19) For the anxious longing of the creation waits eagerly for the revealing of the sons of God . . . . (23) . . . we ourselves, having the first fruits of the Spirit, even we ourselves groan within ourselves, waiting eagerly for our adoption as sons, the redemption of our body."

beautification they will experience at the revelation of Jesus Christ.[121] Neither will I be able to think long upon gospel blessings without thinking also of the infinite glories which will be mine to enjoy in heaven.

Such a gospel-generated heavenward focus yields enormous benefits to me while on earth. The mere hope of seeing Christ in glory releases the purifying influence of heaven upon my life from day to day.[122] Also, knowing of the future love that God will show me in glory enables me to love my fellow-saints with a heaven-inspired love even now.[123] I love others out of the fullness already given to me in Christ, and also out of the greater fullness that will be given to me in glory!

Hope of eternity with Christ in heaven also enables my heart to thrive during the most difficult and lengthy of trials here on earth. When looking at the sheer weight of unseen glories to come, my troubles seem light by comparison; and when looking at the staggering length of eternity, my troubles seem fleeting by comparison.[124] It is only against the backdrop of a glorious eternity that my circumstances can be seen in such a manner; and the promise of this glorious

---

[121]**1 John 3**. "(1) See how great a love the Father has bestowed on us, that we would be called children of God; and such we are. . . . (2) Beloved, now we are children of God, and it has not appeared as yet what we will be. We know that when He appears, we will be like Him, because we will see Him just as He is."

[122]**1 John 3:3**. "And everyone who has this hope fixed on Him, purifies himself, just as He is pure."

[123]**Colossians 1**. "(4) . . . we heard of . . . the love which you have for all the saints; (5) because of the hope laid up for you in heaven, of which you previously heard in the word of truth, the gospel . . ."

[124]**2 Corinthians 4**. "(16) Therefore we do not lose heart, but though our outer man is decaying, yet our inner man is being renewed day by day. (17) For momentary, light affliction is producing for us an eternal weight of glory far beyond all comparison, (18) while we look not at the things which are seen, but at the things which are not seen; for the things which are seen are temporal, but the things which are not seen are eternal."

eternity is part and parcel of the gospel itself.[125]

Preaching the gospel to myself every day is a great way to keep myself established in *"the hope of the gospel,"*[126] so that I might experience the practical benefits that such hope is intended to bring me here on earth.

Mortifying the Flesh with Fullness

Though saved, I am daily beset by a sinful flesh[127] that always craves those things that are contrary to the Spirit.[128] These fleshly lusts are vicious enemies, constantly waging war against the good of my soul.[129] Yet they promise me fullness, and their promises are so deliciously sweet that I often find myself giving into them as if they were friends that have my best interests at heart.

On the most basic of levels, I desire fullness, and fleshly lusts seduce me by attaching themselves to this basic desire. They exploit the empty spaces in me, and they promise that fullness will be mine if I give in to their demands. When my soul sits empty and is aching for something to fill it, such deceptive promises are extremely difficult to resist.

---

[125]**Colossians 1:5.** ". . . the hope laid up for you in heaven, of which you previously heard in the word of truth, the gospel . . . ."

[126]**Colossians 1:23.** ". . . continue in the faith firmly established and steadfast, and not moved away from the hope of the gospel . . . ."

[127]**Galatians 5.** "(19) Now the deeds of the flesh are evident, which are: immorality, impurity, sensuality, (20) idolatry, sorcery, enmities, strife, jealousy, outbursts of anger, disputes, dissensions, factions, (21) envying, drunkenness, carousing, and things like these . . . ."

[128]**Galatians 5:17.** "For the flesh sets its desire against Spirit, and the Spirit against the flesh; for these are in opposition to one another . . . ."

[129]**1 Peter 2:11.** "Beloved, I urge you as aliens and strangers to abstain from fleshly lusts which wage war against the soul."

Consequently, the key to mortifying fleshly lusts is to eliminate the emptiness within me and replace it with fullness; and I accomplish this by feasting on the gospel. Indeed, it is in the gospel that I experience a God who glorifies Himself by filling me with His fullness. He is the One, Paul says, *"who fills all in all."*[130] He is the One who *"fill[s] all things"* with the gifts He gives.[131] And He lavishes gospel blessings upon me with the goal that I *"be filled up to all the fullness of God."*[132] This is the God of the gospel, a God who is satisfied with nothing less than my experience of fullness in Him! The first command God spoke in the Garden was, *"eat freely."*[133] And with similar insistence He says to me now, *"be filled."*[134]

What happens to my appetites for sin when I am filled with the fullness of God in Christ? Jesus provides this answer: *"He who continually comes to Me will never hunger or thirst again."*[135] Indeed, as I perpetually feast on Christ and all of His blessings found in the gospel, I find that my hunger for sin diminishes and the lies of lust simply lose their appeal. Hence, to the degree that I am full, I am free. Eyes do not rove, nor do fleshly lusts rule, when the heart is fat with the love of Jesus!

---

[130]**Ephesians 1**. "(22) . . . the church, (23) which is His body, the fullness of Him who fills all in all."

[131]**Ephesians 4**. "(7) But to each one of us grace was given according to the measure of Christ's gift. (8) Therefore it says, 'When He ascended on high, He led captive a host of captives, and He gave gifts to men.' . . . . (10) . . . He . . . ascended far above all the heavens, so that He might fill all things."

[132]**Ephesians 3**. "(14) For this reason I bow my knees before the Father . . . (16) that He would grant you, according to the riches of His glory . . . (19) . . . that you may be filled up to all the fullness of God."

[133]**Genesis 2:16**. "The Lord God commanded the man, saying, 'From any tree of the garden you may eat freely;'"

[134]**Ephesians 5:18**. ". . . be being filled *[present tense]* by the Spirit." *(literal translation)*

[135]**John 6:35**. "Jesus said to them, 'I am the bread of life; he who is coming *[present tense]* to Me will not hunger, and he who is believing *[present tense]* in Me will never thirst.'" *(literal translation)*

Preaching the gospel to myself each day keeps before me the startling advocacy of God for my fullness, and it also serves as a means by which I feast anew on the fullness of provision that God has given to me in Christ. *"Eat[ing] freely"* of such provision keeps me occupied with God's blessings and also leaves me with a profoundly enjoyable sense of satisfaction in Jesus. And nothing so mortifies fleshly lusts like satisfaction in Him.

Thankfulness Enriched by Relief

The more absorbed I am in the gospel, the more grateful I become in the midst of my circumstances, whatever they may be.

Viewing life's blessings as water in a drinking cup, I know that I could discontentedly focus on the half of the cup that seems empty, or I could gratefully focus on the half that is full. Certainly, the latter approach is the better of the two, yet the gospel cultivates within me a richer gratitude than this.

The gospel reminds me first that what I actually deserve from God is a full cup churning with the torments of His wrath.[136] This is the cup that would be mine to drink if I were given what I deserve each day. With this understanding in mind, I see that to be handed a completely empty cup from God would be cause enough for infinite gratitude. If there were merely the tiniest drop of blessing contained in that otherwise empty cup, I should be blown away by the unbelievable kindness of God toward me. That God,

---

[136]**Revelation 14:10.** "he also will drink of the wine of the wrath of God, which is mixed in full strength in the cup of His anger;" **Psalm 75:8.** "For a cup is in the hand of the Lord, and the wine foams; it is well mixed, and He pours out of this; surely all the wicked of the earth must drain *and* drink down its dregs."

in fact, has given me a cup[137] that is full of *"every spiritual blessing in Christ,"*[138] and this without the slightest admixture of wrath, leaves me truly dumbfounded with inexpressible joy. As for my specific earthly circumstances of plenty or want, I can see them always as infinite improvements on the hell I deserve.

When I look at any circumstance that God apportions me, I am *first* grateful for the wrath I am *not* receiving in that moment (The empty part of the cup never looked so good!). Second, I am grateful for the blessings that are given to me instead of His wrath. (Life's blessings, however small, always appear exceedingly precious when viewed against the backdrop of the wrath I deserve.) This two-layered gratitude disposes my heart to give thanks in all things[139] and it also lends a certain intensity to my giving of thanks. Such a gospel-generated gratitude glorifies God, contributes to peace of mind,[140] and keeps my foot from the path of foolishness and ruin.[141]

---

[137]**Psalm 116.** "(12) What shall I render to the Lord for all His benefits toward me? (13) I shall lift the cup of salvation and call upon the name of the Lord." **Psalm 23:5.** ". . . My cup overflows."

[138]**Ephesians 1:3.** "Blessed be the God and Father of our Lord Jesus Christ, who has blessed us with every spiritual blessing in the heavenly places in Christ,"

[139]**1 Thessalonians 5:18.** "in everything give thanks; for this is God's will for you in Christ Jesus."

[140]**Philippians 4.** "(6) Be anxious for nothing, but in everything by prayer and supplication with thanksgiving let your requests be made known to God. (7) And the peace of God, which surpasses all comprehension, will guard your hearts and your minds in Christ Jesus."

[141]**Romans 1.** "(21) For even though they knew God, they did not honor Him as God or give thanks, but they became futile in their speculations, and their foolish heart was darkened. (22) Professing to be wise, they became fools . . . . (28) And just as they did not see fit to acknowledge God any longer, God gave them over to a depraved mind, to do those things which are not proper, (29) being filled with all unrighteousness, wickedness, greed, evil; full of envy, murder, strife, deceit, malice . . . ."

The Ultimate Prize

In the New Testament, the gospel is several times referred to as *"the gospel of God."*[142] Such an expression should be understood in the fullest sense possible. The gospel is called *"the gospel of God,"* not simply because it is from God, nor merely because it is accomplished through God, but also because ultimately it leads me to God, who is Himself its greatest Prize. Indeed, what makes the gospel such great news is God, who brings me to Himself[143] and then gives Himself so freely to me through Jesus Christ.[144]

The essence of eternal life is not found in having my sins forgiven, in possessing a mansion in heaven, or in having streets of gold on which to walk forever. Rather, the essence of eternal life is intimately knowing God and Jesus Christ whom He has sent.[145] Everything else that God gives to me in the gospel serves merely to bring me to Himself so that this great end might be achieved. Christ died for the forgiveness of my sins so that I might be brought *"to God."*[146] Christ is preparing a place for me in heaven so that He might receive me *"to [Him]self"* and have me forever with Him where He is.[147] And yes, there

---

[142]**Romans 1:1**; **Romans 15:16**; **2 Corinthians 11:7**; **1 Thessalonians 2:2,8,9**; **1 Peter 4:17**.

[143]**Ephesians 1**. "(4) . . . He chose us in Him . . . that we should be . . . before Him . . . . (5) He predestined us to adoption as sons . . . to Himself . . . ."

[144]**Romans 5:5**. ". . . the love of God has been poured out within our hearts through the Holy Spirit who was given to us." **John 14:21**. ". . . he who loves Me will be loved by My Father, and I will love him and will disclose Myself to him."

[145]**John 17:3**. "This is eternal life, that they may know You, the only true God, and Jesus Christ whom You have sent."

[146]**1 Peter 3:18**. "For Christ also died for sins once for all . . . so that He might bring us to God . . . ."

[147]**John 14**. "(2) In My Father's house are many dwelling places . . . . I go to prepare a place for you. (3) If I go and prepare a place for you, I will come again and receive you to Myself, that where I am, there you may be also."

is a great street of gold in heaven, but is there any doubt where the street leads? Unquestionably, it leads straight to the throne of God Himself,[148] as do all of God's gifts to me in the gospel.

As I meditate on the gospel each day, I find my thoughts inevitably traveling from the gifts I've received to the Giver of those gifts; and the more my thoughts are directed to Him, the more I experience the essence of eternal life. The *"gospel of God"* is from God, comes through God, and leads me to God;[149] and it is in Him that my soul finds its truest joy and rest.[150]

My Manifesto

Boldness is critical. Without boldness, my life story will be one of great deeds left undone, victories left unwon, petitions left unprayed, and timely words unsaid. If I wish to live only a pathetically small portion of the life God has prepared for me, then I need no boldness. But if I want my life to bloom full and loom large for the glory of God, then I must have boldness – and nothing so nourishes boldness in me like the gospel!

The gospel gives me boldness first by banishing my greatest fear, the fear of God's eternal wrath. Indeed, Christ bore God's wrath upon Himself, not simply so I could escape

---

[148]**Revelation.** "(21:21) . . . . And the street of the city was pure gold . . . . (22:1) Then he showed me a river of the water of life . . . coming from the throne of God and of the Lamb, (2) in the middle of its street. . . ."

[149]**Romans 11:36.** "For from Him and through Him and to Him are all things. To Him be the glory forever. Amen."

[150]**Psalm 16:11.** ". . . in Your presence is fullness of joy; in your right hand there are pleasures forever." **Psalm 37:4.** "Delight yourself in the Lord; and He will give you the desires of your heart." **Psalm 73.** "(25) . . . besides You, I desire nothing on earth. (26) . . . God is . . . my portion forever . . . . (28) . . . the nearness of God is my good . . . ."

that wrath on some future day, but also that I might be released from the daily fear of such wrath as I think ahead to judgment day. Because this fear hinders the ongoing work of God in me, the love of God continually expels this fear (whenever it appears) and nurtures within me a confident eagerness to face God on judgment day.[151] Living in the daily relief of this fear frees me up to continue being perfected in confidence by the love of God, and it also serves to put all other fears, especially the fear of man, into perspective.[152]

Additionally, the more I experience the life-transforming power of the gospel, the more confident I am in speaking it to others, both saved and lost.[153] I know what the gospel can do in people's lives if they would believe the fullness of it, because I see what it is doing in me and in others. Therefore, I have increasing boldness to speak the whole gospel to others,[154] even amid opposition.[155]

Also, the more I comprehend what God has done for me through Christ, the more I find myself confidently coming

---

[151]**1 John 4.** "(17) By this, love is perfected with us, so that we may have confidence in the day of judgment; because as He is, so also are we in this world. (18) There is no fear in love; but perfect love casts out fear, because fear involves punishment, and the one who fears is not perfected in love."

[152]**Matthew 10:28.** "Do not fear those who kill the body but are unable to kill the soul; but rather fear Him who is able to destroy both soul and body in hell."

[153]**Romans 1.** "(15) So, for my part, I am eager to preach the gospel to you also who are in Rome. (16) For I am not ashamed of the gospel, for it is the power of God for salvation to everyone who believes . . . ." **1 Corinthians 1:18.** ". . . to us who are being saved it [the word of the cross] is the power of God."

[154]**Acts 20.** "(26) Therefore, I testify to you this day that I am innocent of the blood of all men. (27) For I did not shrink from declaring to you the whole purpose of God."

[155]**Acts 4.** "(29) And now, Lord, take note of their threats, and grant that Your bond-servants may speak Your word with all confidence, ... (31) And when they had prayed, . . . they were all filled with the Holy Spirit and began to speak the word of God with boldness."

before God in prayer,[156] speaking to Him in situations in which I formerly would have shrunk from Him, and offering requests that I formerly would have been too timid to offer (due either to the largeness of the request or my own sinful unworthiness). With greater boldness in prayer comes an increased enjoyment of God and the bounty that He gives, due simply to the fact that I was daring enough to ask for what was needed.[157]

Preaching the gospel to myself each day nourishes within me a holy brazenness to believe what God says, enjoy what He offers, and do what He commands. Admittedly, I don't deserve to be a child of God and I don't deserve to be free of sin's guilt and power. I don't deserve the staggering privilege of intimacy with God, nor any other blessing that Christ has purchased for me with His blood. I don't even deserve to be useful to God. But by the grace of God I am what I am and I have what I have, and I hereby resolve not to let any portion of God's grace prove vain in me![158] And to the degree that I fail to live up to this resolve, I will boldly take for myself the forgiveness that God says is mine and continue walking in His grace. This is my manifesto, my daily resolve; and may God be glorified by this confidence that I place in Him.

---

[156]**Hebrews 4:16.** "Therefore let us draw near with confidence to the throne of grace, so that we may receive mercy and find grace to help in time of need." **Hebrews 10**. "(19) Therefore, brethren, since we have confidence to enter the holy place by the blood of Jesus, (20) by a new and living way which He inaugurated for us through the veil, that is, His flesh, (21) and since we have a great priest over the house of God, (22) let us draw near with a sincere heart in full assurance of faith . . . ."

[157]**James 4:2.** ". . . . You do not have because you do not ask."

[158]**1 Corinthians 15**. "(9) For I am the least of the apostles, and not fit to be called an apostle, because I persecuted the church of God. (10) But by the grace of God I am what I am, and His grace toward me did not prove vain; but I labored even more than all of them, yet not I, but the grace of God with me."

To Him be the Glory

"*To the praise of the glory of His grace . . . to the praise of His glory . . . to the praise of His glory.*"[159] These refrains fly as banners over the gospel truths parading through the early verses of Ephesians. They herald the ultimate motive of God in all His gospel acts on behalf of those whom He has saved. They also announce the effect which the gospel will most certainly wield upon those who experience its fullness. It is no surprise, then, that the Apostle ends his gospel review in Ephesians 3 by bowing his knees in worship and ascribing all glory to God.[160] "*Unto Him be the glory,*" Paul exclaims at the end of Ephesians 3. "*To . . . Him be the glory,*" he cries after his gospel meditations through Romans.[161] "*To the King . . . be glory,*" he urges in 1 Timothy after speaking of God's merciful saving of him.[162] Clearly, the gospel generated in

---

[159]**Ephesians 1.** "(5) He predestined us to adoption as sons . . . (6) to the praise of the glory of His grace . . . . (10) . . . . In Him (11) also we have obtained an inheritance . . . (12) to the end that we . . . would be to the praise of His glory. (13) In Him, you also, after listening to the message of truth, the gospel of your salvation – having also believed, you were sealed in Him with the Holy Spirit . . . , (14) who is given as a pledge of our inheritance, with a view to the redemption of God's own possession, to the praise of His glory."

[160]**Ephesians 3.** "(14) For this reason I bow my knees before the Father . . . . (20) Now to Him who is able to do far more abundantly beyond all that we ask or think, according to the power that works within us, (21) to Him be the glory in the church and in Christ Jesus to all generations forever and ever. Amen."

[161]**Romans 11.** "(33) Oh, the depth of the riches both of the wisdom and knowledge of God! How unsearchable are His judgments and unfathomable His ways! (34) For who has known the mind of the Lord, or who became His counselor? (35) Or who has first given to Him that it might be paid back to him again? (36) For from Him and through Him and to Him are all things. To Him be the glory forever. Amen."

[162]**1 Timothy 1.** "(15) . . . Christ Jesus came into the world to save sinners, among whom I am foremost of all. (16) Yet for this reason I found mercy, so that in me as the foremost, Jesus Christ might demonstrate His perfect patience as an example for those who would believe in Him for eternal life. (17) Now to the King eternal, immortal, invisible, the only God, be honor and glory forever and ever. Amen."

Paul an enormous passion for God's glory; and the gospel does the same in me as I make it the meditation of my heart each day.

Understanding that I am not the ultimate end of the gospel, but rather that God's glory is, actually enables me to embrace my salvation more boldly than I would otherwise dare to do. For example, when my timid heart questions why God would want to love one so sinful as I, I read the answer, *"to the praise of the glory of His grace."* I figure, then, that my unworthiness must actually be useful to God, because it magnifies the degree to which His grace might be glorified as He lavishes His saving kindness upon me. This line of reasoning makes perfect sense to me and convinces me to embrace the gospel with greater passion so that God might glorify Himself through me, an unworthy sinner.

Indeed, the more I embrace and experience the gospel, the more I delight in the worship of God, the more expressive my joy in Him becomes, and the more I yearn to glorify Him in all I say and do.[163]

---

[163] **1 Peter 1.** "(6) In this [salvation] you greatly rejoice . . . (8) . . . you greatly rejoice with a joy inexpressible and full of glory, (9) obtaining as the outcome of your faith the salvation of your souls." **1 Corinthians 10:31.** "Whether, then, you eat or drink or whatever you do, do all to the glory of God."

PART II

A Gospel Narrative

Prose Version

"To use an expression . . . , we must 'preach the gospel to ourselves every day.' For me that means I keep going back to Scriptures such as Isaiah 53:6, Galatians 2:20, and Romans 8:1. It means I frequently repeat the words from an old hymn, 'My hope is built on nothing less than Jesus' blood and righteousness.'"

Jerry Bridges, in *"Gospel-Driven Sanctification"*

The Glory of God

1 My God is immense beyond imagination. He measured the entire universe with merely the span of His hand.[164]

2 He is unimaginably awesome in all of His perfections, absolutely righteous, holy, and just in all of His ways.[165]

3 He has also been unbelievably good and merciful to me as the Creator and Sustainer of my life.

4 Every breath, every heartbeat, every function of every organ in my body is a gift from Him.

5 Every legitimate pleasure I experience is a gift from His loving hand to me.[166]

6 All that I am and all that I have I owe to Him and to His goodness.[167]

7 My life in every way is, and will continue to be, utterly dependent upon Him in whom I live and move and have my being.[168]

---

[164]**Isaiah 40:12.** "Who has measured the waters in the hollow of His hand, and marked off the heavens by the span . . . ?" *[a 'span' is a hand breadth]*

[165]**Deuteronomy 32.** "(3) For I proclaim the name of the Lord; Ascribe greatness to our God! (4) The Rock! His work is perfect, for all His ways are just; A God of faithfulness and without injustice, righteous and upright is He."

[166]**1 Timothy 6:17.** ". . . God . . . richly supplies us with all things to enjoy." **Acts 14:17.** "and yet He did not leave Himself without witness, in that He did good and gave you rains from heaven and fruitful seasons, satisfying your hearts with food and gladness."

[167]**James 1:17.** "Every good thing given and every perfect gift is from above, coming down from the Father of lights, with whom there is no variation or shifting shadow."

[168]**Acts 17:28.** "for in Him we live and move and exist . . . ."

8 This wonderful God is the most supremely worthy Object of admiration,[169] honor,[170] and delight[171] in all of the universe;

9 And He has created me with the intention that I might glorify Him[172] by finding my soul's delight in Him and by living in joyful obedience to Him in all of my ways.[173]

My Sin Against God

10 Yet I could not have failed this great God more miserably than I have.[174]

---

[169]**Psalm 96.** "(3) Tell of His glory among the nations, His wonderful deeds among the peoples. (4) For great is the Lord and greatly to be praised; He is to be feared above all gods. (5) For all the gods of the peoples are idols, but the Lord made the heavens. (6) Splendor and majesty are before Him, strength and beauty are in His sanctuary. (7) . . . Ascribe to the Lord glory and strength. (8) Ascribe to the Lord the glory of His name . . . ."

[170]**Revelation 4:11.** "Worthy are You, our Lord and our God, to receive glory and honor and power; for You created all things, and because of Your will they existed, and were created."

[171]**Psalm 16:11.** ". . . . in Your presence is fullness of joy; In Your right hand there are pleasures forever." **Psalm 37:4.** "Delight yourself in the Lord . . . ."

[172]**Romans 11:36.** "For from Him and through Him and to Him are all things [including me]. To Him be the glory forever. Amen." **1 Corinthians 10:31.** "Whether, then, you eat or drink or whatever you do, do all to the glory of God."

[173]**Psalm 37:4.** "Delight yourself in the Lord . . . ." **Deuteronomy 5.** "(28) . . . the Lord said . . . , '(29) Oh that they had such a heart in them, that they would fear Me and keep all My commandments always, that it may be well with them and with their sons forever!'"

[174]**Romans 1.** "(21) For even though they knew God, they did not honor Him as God or give thanks, but they became futile in their speculations, and their foolish heart was darkened. (22) Professing to be wise, they became fools, (23) and exchanged the glory of the incorruptible God for an image in the form of corruptible man . . . . (25) . . . they exchanged the truth of God for a lie, and worshiped and served the creature rather than the Creator . . . ." **Romans 3:23.** "For all have sinned and fall short of the glory of God,"

11 Instead of giving thanks to Him and humbly submitting to His rule over my life, I have rebelled against Him and have actually sought to exalt myself above Him.

12 Going my own way and living according to my own wisdom, I have broken countless times either the letter or the spirit of every one of God's Ten Commandments.[175]

13 Thinking myself to be wise, I have shown myself to be a fool; and because of my arrogance, God has every right to damn me to the everlasting experience of His terrifying wrath in the Lake of Fire.[176]

14 So as for myself, apart from Christ I am bound by the guilt of my sins[177] and also bound by the power of sin, enslaved to various lusts and pleasures.[178]

---

[175]**Exodus 20.** "'(3) You shall have no other gods before Me. (4) You shall not make for yourself an idol . . . . (7) You shall not take the name of the Lord your God in vain . . . (8) Remember the sabbath day, to keep it holy, (12) Honor your father and your mother . . . . (13) You shall not murder. (14) You shall not commit adultery. (15) You shall not steal. (16) You shall not bear false witness against your neighbor. (17) You shall not covet . . anything that belongs to your neighbor." **Colossians 3:5.** ". . . greed . . . amounts to idolatry." **Matthew 5.** "(27) You have heard that it was said, 'You shall not commit adultery'; (28) but I say to you that everyone who looks at a woman with lust for her has already committed adultery with her in his heart." **1 John 3:15** "Everyone who hates his brother is a murderer; and you know that no murderer has eternal life abiding in him."

[176]**Romans 6:23.** "For the wages of sin is death . . . ." **Revelation 21:8.** "But for the cowardly and unbelieving and abominable and murderers and immoral persons and sorcerers and idolaters and all liars, their part will be in the lake that burns with fire and brimstone, which is the second death." **Ephesians 2:3.** ". . . we too all formerly lived in the lusts of our flesh, indulging the desires of the flesh and of the mind, and were by nature children of wrath, even as the rest."

[177]**Romans 3:19.** "Now we know that whatever the Law says, it says to those who are under the law, that every mouth may be stopped, and all the world may become guilty before God." *(New King James Version)* **James 2:10.** "For whoever keeps the whole law and yet stumbles in one point, he has become guilty of all."

[178]**Titus 3:3.** "For we also once were foolish ourselves, disobedient, deceived, enslaved to various lusts and pleasures, spending our life in malice and envy, hateful, hating one another." **Ephesians 2:3.** ". . . we too all formerly lived in the lusts of our flesh, indulging the desires of the flesh and of the mind . . . ."

15 Apart from Christ, I am also utterly deserving of and destined for eternal punishment in the Lake of Fire, completely unable to save myself or even to make one iota of a contribution to my own salvation.[179]

God's Work on My Behalf

16 However, what I could not do, God did[180] – and in doing it, He did it all, sending His own Son into the world to die on the cross for my sins,[181] thereby showing me unfathomable love.[182]

17 God loved me so much that He was willing to suffer the loss of His Son,[183] and even more amazingly, He was willing to allow His Son to suffer the loss of Him at the cross.[184]

18 Jesus loved me so much that He was willing to lay down His life for me. No one could ever love me more or

---

[179]**Romans 5:6.** ". . . we were . . . helpless . . . ."

[180]**Romans 5:6.** "For while we were still helpless, at the right time Christ died for the ungodly."

[181]**Romans 8:3.** "For what the Law could not do, weak as it was through the flesh, God did: sending His own Son in the likeness of sinful flesh and as an offering for sin, He condemned sin in the flesh," **1 Peter 3:18.** "For Christ also died for sins once for all, the just for the unjust, in order that He might bring us to God . . . ."

[182]**Romans 5.** "(7) For one will hardly die for a righteous man; though perhaps for the good man someone would dare even to die. (8) But God demonstrates His own love toward us, in that while we were yet sinners, Christ died for us."

[183]**John 3:16.** "For God so loved the world, that He gave His only begotten Son . . . ." **Romans 8:32.** "He . . . did not spare His own Son, but delivered Him over for us all . . . ."

[184]**Mark 15:34.** "And at the ninth hour Jesus cried out with a loud voice, . . . 'My God, my God, why have You forsaken Me?'"

better than Jesus.[185]

19 On the third day after Jesus' death, God raised Him from the dead,[186] thereby announcing that His death was completely sufficient to atone for every sin that I have or will commit throughout my lifetime.[187]

20 God then exalted Christ to His own right hand,[188] where Christ now reigns from on high, granting salvation and forgiveness[189] to all who call on Him by faith.[190]

My Salvation

21 Now when my time came and I placed my faith in Jesus, God instantly granted me a great salvation.

22 He forgave me of all of my sins, past, present, and future.[191]

---

[185]**John 15**. "(12) . . . I have loved you. (13) Greater love has no one than this, that one lay down his life for his friends. (14) You are My friends . . . ."

[186]**1 Corinthians 15:4**. ". . . He was raised on the third day according to the Scriptures,"

[187]**Acts 13**. "(30) But God raised Him from the dead . . . . (38) Therefore let it be known to you, brethren, that through Him forgiveness of sins is proclaimed to you, (39) and through Him everyone who believes is freed from all things, from which you could not be freed through the Law of Moses."

[188]**Ephesians 1**. "(20) . . . He [God] raised Him [Jesus] from the dead, and seated Him at His right hand in the heavenly places, (21) far above all rule and authority and power and dominion, and every name that is named, not only in this age, but also in the one to come."

[189]**Acts 5:31**. "He [Jesus] is the one whom God exalted to His right hand as a Prince and a Savior, to grant repentance . . . and forgiveness of sins."

[190]**Romans 10**. "(13) for whoever will call on the name of the Lord will be saved. (14) How then will they call on Him in whom they have not believed?" **Acts 16:31**. "They said, 'Believe in the Lord Jesus, and you will be saved . . . .'"

[191]**Colossians 2:13**. ". . . He made you alive together with Him, having forgiven us all our transgressions," **Psalm 103:12**. "As far as the east is from the west, so far has He removed our transgressions from us."

23 He made me His child, adopting me into His family.[192]

24 He gave me the gift of the Holy Spirit, who gives me God's power,[193] who pours out God's love within my heart,[194] and who tenderly communicates to my spirit that I am a child of God and an heir of eternal glory in heaven.[195]

25 In saving me, God also freed me from slavery to any and all sins.[196]

26 I no longer have to sin again, for sin's mastery over me has been broken!

27 In saving me, God also justified me,[197] and being justified through Christ, I have a peace with God that will endure forever.

28 In justifying me, God declared me innocent of my sins and pronounced me righteous with the very righteousness of Jesus.[198]

---

[192]**Ephesians 1:5.** "He predestined us to adoption as sons through Jesus Christ to Himself . . . ." **John 1:12.** "But as many as received Him, to them He gave the right to become children of God, even to those who believe in His name,"

[193]**Acts 1:8.** ". . . you will receive power when the Holy Spirit has come upon you . . . ." **Ephesians 3:16.** "that He would grant you . . . to be strengthened with power through His Spirit in the inner man,"

[194]**Ephesians 1.** "(13) . . . you were sealed in Him with the Holy Spirit of promise, (14) who is given as a pledge of our inheritance. . . ." **Romans 5:5.** " . . . the love of God is poured out within our hearts through the Holy Spirit who is given to us."

[195]**Romans 8.** "(16) The Spirit Himself testifies with our spirit that we are children of God, (17) and if children, heirs also, heirs of God and fellow heirs with Christ . . . ."

[196]**Romans 6.** "(6) knowing this, that our old self was crucified with Him, in order that our body of sin might be done away with, so that we would no longer be slaves to sin; (7) for he who has died is freed from sin. . . . (14) For sin shall not be master over you, for you are not under law but under grace."

[197]**Romans 5:1.** "Therefore, having been justified by faith, we have peace with God through our Lord Jesus Christ,"

[198]**Romans 5:18.** "So then as through one transgression there resulted condemnation to all men, even so through one act of righteousness there resulted justification of life to all men."

29 God also allowed His future and present wrath against me to be completely propitiated by Jesus, who bore it upon Himself while on the cross.[199]

30 Consequently, God now has only love, compassion, and deepest affection for me, and this love is without any admixture of wrath whatsoever.

31 God always looks upon me and treats me with gracious favor, always working all things together for my ultimate and eternal good.[200]

32 God's grace abounds to me even through trials.

33 Because I am a justified one, He subjugates every trial and forces it to do good unto me.[201]

34 When I sin, God's grace abounds to me all the more as He graciously maintains my justified status as described above.[202]

35 When I sin, God feels no wrath in His heart against me.[203]

---

[199] **1 John 2:2.** ". . . He [Christ] Himself is the propitiation for our sins . . . ." *('propitiation' = satisfaction, appeasement of wrath)*

[200] **Romans 8:28.** "And we know that God causes all things to work together for good to those who love God, to those who are called according to His purpose."

[201] **Romans 5.** "(1) Therefore, having been justified by faith, we have peace with God through our Lord Jesus Christ, (2) through whom also we have obtained our introduction by faith into this grace in which we stand; and we exult in hope of the glory of God. (3) And not only this, but we also exult in our tribulations, knowing that tribulation brings about perseverance; (4) and perseverance, proven character; and proven character, hope; (5) and hope does not disappoint, because the love of God has been poured out within our hearts through the Holy Spirit who was given to us."

[202] **Romans 5.** "(20) . . . where sin increased, grace abounded all the more, (21) so that, as sin reigned in death, even so grace would reign through righteousness to eternal life through Jesus Christ our Lord."

[203] **I Thessalonians 5.** "(9) For God has not destined us for wrath, but for obtaining salvation through our Lord Jesus Christ, (10) who died for us, so that whether we are awake or asleep, we will live together with Him."
1 John 2:2. ". . . He [Christ] Himself is the propitiation for our sins . . ." *('propitiation' = satisfaction, appeasement of wrath)*

36 His heart is filled with nothing but love for me, and He longs for me to repent and confess my sins to Him, so that He might show me the gracious and forgiving love that has been in His heart all along.[204]

37 God does not require my confession before He desires to forgive me.

38 In His heart He already has forgiven me; and when I come to Him to confess my sins to Him, He runs to me (as it were) and is repeatedly embracing and kissing me even before I get the words of my confession out of my mouth![205]

39 God does see my sins, and He is grieved by my sins.[206] His grief comes partly from the fact that in my moments of sin, I am not receiving the fullness of His love for me.

---

[204]**1 John 1:9.** "If we confess our sins, He is faithful and righteous to forgive us our sins and to cleanse us from all unrighteousness."

[205]**Luke 15.** "(20) So he got up and came to his father. But while he was still a long way off, his father saw him and felt compassion for him, and ran and embraced him and kissed him. (21) And the son said to him, 'Father, I have sinned against heaven and in your sight; I am no longer worthy to be called your son.' (22) But the father said to his slaves, 'Quickly bring out the best robe and put it on him, and put a ring on his hand and sandals on his feet; (23) and bring the fattened calf, kill it, and let us eat and celebrate; (24) for this son of mine was dead and has come to life again; he was lost and has been found.' And they began to celebrate."

[206]**Ephesians 4:30.** "Do not grieve the Holy Spirit of God . . . ."

40 He even sends chastisement into my life;[207] but He does so because He is for me,[208] and He loves me;[209] and He disciplines me for my ultimate good.[210]

41 I don't deserve any of this, even on my best day; but this is my salvation, and herein I stand.[211] Thank You, Jesus.

---

[207]**Hebrews 12**. "(5) and you have forgotten the exhortation which is addressed to you as sons, 'My son, do not regard lightly the discipline of the Lord, nor faint when you are reproved by Him; (6) For those whom the Lord loves He disciplines, and He scourges every son whom He receives.' (7) It is for discipline that you endure; God deals with you as with sons; for what son is there whom his father does not discipline? (8) But if you are without discipline, of which we all have become partakers, then you are illegitimate children and not sons. (9) Furthermore, we had earthly fathers to discipline us, and we respected them; shall we not much rather be subject to the Father of spirits, and live?"

[208]**Romans 8:31**. ". . . God is for us . . . ."

[209]**Hebrews 12:6**. "For those whom the Lord loves He disciplines, and He scourges every son whom He receives."

[210]**Hebrews 12:10**. "For they disciplined us for a short time as seemed best to them, but He disciplines us for our good, so that we may share His holiness."

[211]**1 Peter 5:12**. ". . . this is the true grace of God. Stand firm in it!" **1 Corinthians 16:13**. ". . . stand firm in the faith . . . ." **Colossians 1:23**. ". . . continue in the faith firmly established and steadfast, and not moved away from the hope of the gospel . . . ."

PART III

A Gospel Narrative

Poetic Version

"Never be content with your current grasp of the gospel. The gospel is life-permeating, world-altering, universe-changing truth. It has more facets than a diamond. Its depths man will never exhaust."

C.J. Mahaney, *The Cross Centered Life*, 67

Beholding the heavens,
 I now understand
God measured them all
  with the breadth of His hand.[212]
He fashioned the trillions
 of stars in the sky,[213]
The sun and the moon
 He established on high.[214]
All heaven and earth,
 which He made in six days,[215]
Show daily and nightly
 His merit of praise.[216]

---

[212]**Isaiah 40:12.** "Who has measured the waters in the hollow of His hand, and marked off the heavens by the span . . . ?" *[a 'span' is a hand breadth]*

[213]**Isaiah 40:26.** "Lift up your eyes on high and see who has created these stars, the One who leads forth their host by number, He calls them all by name; because of the greatness of His might and the strength of His power, not one of them is missing."

[214]**Psalm 8.** "(3) When I consider Your heavens, the work of Your fingers, the moon and the stars which You have ordained, (4) what is man that You take thought of him, and the son of man that You care for him?"

[215]**Exodus 20:11.** "For in six days the Lord made the heavens and the earth . . ."

[216]**Psalm 19.** "(1) The heavens are telling the glory of God; and their expanse is declaring the work of His hands. (2) Day to day pours forth speech, and night to night reveals knowledge."

So wondrously caring[217]

is God ev'ry day,

Creating,[218] sustaining

my life ev'ry way.[219]

Each breath I intake,

ev'ry beat of my heart,

All pleasures well-tasted

are His to impart.[220]

Indeed, for such blessings

He should be adored

And honored supremely

as eminent Lord.[221]

---

[217] **1 Peter 5:7**. ". . . He cares for you."

[218] **Psalm 139**. "(13) For You formed my inward parts; You wove me in my mother's womb. (14) I will give thanks to You, for I am fearfully and wonderfully made; wonderful are Your works, and my soul knows it very well. (15) My frame was not hidden from You, when I was made in secret, *and* skillfully wrought in the depths of the earth; (16) Your eyes have seen my unformed substance; and in Your book were all written the days that were ordained for me, when as yet there was not one of them."

[219] **Acts 17**. "(27) . . . He is not far from each one of us; (28) for in Him we live and move and exist . . . ."

[220] **1 Timothy 6:17**. "God . . . richly supplies us with all things to enjoy." **Acts 14:17**. "And yet He did not leave Himself without witness, in that He did good and gave you rains from heaven and fruitful seasons, satisfying your hearts with food and gladness."

[221] **Revelation 4:11**. "Worthy are You, our Lord and our God, to receive glory and honor and power; for You created all things, and because of Your will they existed, and were created."

In fact, for this purpose

He brought me to be,

That I might His glory

and kindliness see[222]

And cherish Him fully

in all of my days,[223]

Obeying with pleasure

whatever He says,[224]

Fulfilling the calling

He's laid upon me

To show forth His glory

deliberately.[225]

---

[222]**Romans 2:4.** "Or do you think lightly of the riches of His kindness and tolerance and patience, not knowing that the kindness of God leads you to repentance?"

[223]**Luke 10:27.** "And he answered, 'You shall love the Lord your God with all your heart, and with all your soul, and with all your strength, and with all your mind . . . .'"

[224]**John 14.** "(15) If you love Me, you will keep My commandments. . . . (21) He who has My commandments and keeps them is the one who loves Me . . . ." **1 John 5:3.** "For this is the love of God, that we keep His commandments; and His commandments are not burdensome."

[225]**Romans 11:36.** "For from Him and through Him and to Him are all things *[including me]*. To Him be the glory forever. Amen." **1 Corinthians 10:31.** "Whether, then, you eat or drink or whatever you do, do all to the glory of God."

Yet I could not fail God

    much worse than I've done.

Ignoring His glory,

    for mine I have run.

I've spurned a life

    under His wisdom and care,

Begrudged Him the throne

    and pretended me there.[226]

A prideful and lust-laden

    path I have trod,

Transgressing all Ten great

    Commandments of God.[227]

---

[226]**Romans 1:21.** "For even though they knew God, they did not honor Him as God or give thanks, but they became futile in their speculations, and their foolish heart was darkened. (22) Professing to be wise, they became fools, (23) and exchanged the glory of the incorruptible God for an image in the form of corruptible man . . . . (25) . . . they exchanged the truth of God for a lie, and worshiped and served the creature rather than the Creator, who is blessed forever. Amen." **Romans 3:23.** "For all have sinned and fall short of the glory of God."

[227]**Exodus 20.** "'(3) You shall have no other gods before Me. (4) You shall not make for yourself an idol . . . . (7) You shall not take the name of the Lord your God in vain . . . (8) Remember the sabbath day, to keep it holy, (12) Honor your father and your mother . . . . (13) You shall not murder. (14) You shall not commit adultery. (15) You shall not steal. (16) You shall not bear false witness against your neighbor. (17) You shall not covet . . . anything that belongs to your neighbor." **Colossians 3:5.** ". . . greed . . . amounts to idolatry." **Matthew 5.** "(27) You have heard that it was said, 'You shall not commit adultery'; (28) but I say to you that everyone who looks at a woman with lust for her has already committed adultery with her in his heart." **1 John 3:15.** "Everyone who hates his brother is a murderer; and you know that no murderer has eternal life abiding in him."

My foolish rebellion
　　gives God ev'ry right
To damn me with haste
　　to the mis'rable plight
Of terrible judgments
　　in His Lake of Fire,[228]
Where wrath is most fierce
　　and will never expire.[229]
With wickedest sinners
　　I truly should know
The worst of Hell's furies
　　for failing God so.

---

[228]**Romans 6:23.** "For the wages of sin is death . . . ." **Revelation 21:8.** "But for the cowardly and unbelieving and abominable and murderers and immoral persons and sorcerers and idolaters and all liars, their part will be in the lake that burns with fire and brimstone, which is the second death." **Ephesians 2:3.** " . . . we too all formerly lived in the lusts of our flesh, indulging the desires of the flesh and of the mind, and were by nature children of wrath, even as the rest."

[229]**Matthew 25:46.** "These will go away into eternal punishment, but the righteous into eternal life." **Mark 9.** "(47) If your eye causes you to stumble, throw it out; it is better for you to enter the kingdom of God with one eye, than, having two eyes, to be cast into hell, (48) where their worm does not die, and the fire is not quenched."

So this is my status
  and these are my flaws
Apart from Christ Jesus
  and His saving cause:
I carry sin's guilt
  and am gripped by sin's pow'r,[230]
Held fast to its
  various lusts ev'ry hour,[231]
Deserving of flames,
  both within and without,[232]
And sliding t'ward Hell
  as I toss all about,[233]

---

[230]**Romans 6.** "(16) Do you not know that when you present yourselves to someone as slaves for obedience, you are slaves of the one whom you obey, either of sin resulting in death, or of obedience resulting in righteousness? (17) . . . you were slaves of sin . . . . (20) . . . you were slaves of sin . . . ."

[231]**Titus 3:3.** "For we also once were foolish ourselves, disobedient, deceived, enslaved to various lusts and pleasures, spending our life in malice and envy, hateful, hating one another."

[232]**Revelation 21:8.** "But for the cowardly and unbelieving and abominable and murderers and immoral persons and sorcerers and idolaters and all liars, their part will be in the lake that burns with fire and brimstone, which is the second death."

[233]**Isaiah 57.** "(20) But the wicked are like the tossing sea, for it cannot be quiet, and its waters toss up refuse and mud. (21) 'There is no peace,' says my God, 'for the wicked.'"

Too reprobate[234] even
    to play a small part
In clearing my record
    or changing my heart[235]
To pacify wrath
    and be worthy of grace,
To make myself lovely[236]
    and win God's embrace.
Completely condemned by
    God's Law in its whole,[237]
I've nothing to offer
    to ransom my soul.[238]

---

[234]**reprobate.** *adj.* under God's judgment, extremely sinful, lost in sin.

[235]**Jeremiah 17:9.** "The heart is more deceitful than all else and is desperately sick; who can understand it?" **Mark 7.** "(21) For from within, out of the heart of men, proceed the evil thoughts, fornications, thefts, murders, adulteries, (22) deeds of coveting and wickedness, as well as deceit, sensuality, envy, slander, pride and foolishness. (23) All these evil things proceed from within and defile the man."

[236]**Isaiah 64:6.** "For all of us have become like one who is unclean, and all our righteous deeds are like a filthy garment . . . ."

[237]**James 2:10.** "For whoever keeps the whole law, and yet stumbles in one point, he has become guilty of all."

[238]**Romans 5:6.** ". . . we were . . . helpless . . . ."

But wonder of wonders,

    so great to behold,[239]

My God chose to save me[240]

    with method so bold.

What I could not render,

    God fully has done,

And doing, He rendered it

    all through His Son.[241]

He sent Christ to die

    on the cross for my sin

To suffer my anguish,

    my pardon to win.[242]

---

[239]**1 Peter 1.** "(10) As to this salvation, the prophets who prophesied of the grace that would come to you made careful searches and inquiries, (11) seeking to know what person or time the Spirit of Christ within them was indicating as He predicted the sufferings of Christ and the glories to follow. (12) It was revealed to them that they were not serving themselves, but you, in these things which now have been announced to you through those who preached the gospel to you by the Holy Spirit sent from heaven – things into which angels long to look."

[240]**Ephesians 1.** "(4) . . . He chose us in Him before the foundation of the world, that we would be holy and blameless before Him. In love (5) He predestined us to adoption as sons through Jesus Christ to Himself . . . ."

[241]**Acts 4:12.** "And there is salvation in no one else; for there is no other name under heaven that has been given among men, by which we must be saved." **John 14:6.** "Jesus said to him, 'I am the way, the truth, and the life; no one comes to the Father but through Me.'"

[242]**1 Peter 3:18.** "For Christ also died for our sins once for all, the just for the unjust, so that He might bring us to God . . . ." **1 Corinthians 15:3.** ". . . Christ died for our sins . . . ."

Amazing it is, when I
stop to regard,
That God would consent
to an anguish so hard,
Surrend'ring His Son[243]
unto mayhem and death,[244]
To torturous writhing
'til His final breath.
'Why does God forsake Me?'
alone Jesus cried;[245]
Yet God left Him hanging
until He had died.

---

[243]**Romans 8:32.** "He . . . did not spare His own Son, but delivered Him over for us all . . . ." **John 3:16.** "For God so loved the world, that He gave His only begotten Son, that whoever believes in Him shall not perish, but have eternal life."

[244]**Isaiah 53.** "(3) He was despised and forsaken of men, a man of sorrows and acquainted with grief . . . (4) . . . our griefs He Himself bore, and our sorrows He carried . . . . (5) . . . He was pierced through for our transgressions, He was crushed for our iniquities; the chastening for our well-being fell upon Him . . . . (6) . . . the Lord has caused the iniquity of us all to fall on Him. (7) He was oppressed and He was afflicted . . . . (8) By oppression and judgment He was taken away . . . He was cut off out of the land of the living . . . . (10) . the Lord was pleased to crush Him, putting Him to grief . . . ." **Acts 2:23.** "this Man [Jesus], delivered over by the predetermined plan and foreknowledge of God, you nailed to a cross by the hands of godless men and put Him to death."

[245]**Mark 15:34.** "At the ninth hour Jesus cried out with a loud voice, . . . 'My God, my God, why have You forsaken Me?'"

That Jesus was willing

    His life to lay down,[246]

Be scourged[247] and insulted

    and wear thorny crown[248]

For one such as I

    who had spited God so,

Amazes and blesses

    and makes me to know

That greater a lover

    is no man than He,

Who laid down His life

    for a sinner like me.[249]

---

[246] **John 10**. "(17) For this reason the Father loves Me, because I lay down My life . . . . (18) No one has taken it away from Me, but I lay it down on My own initiative . . . ."

[247] **John 19:1**. "Pilate then took Jesus and scourged Him."

[248] **Mark 15**. "(17) They dressed Him up in purple, and after twisting a crown of thorns, they put it on Him; (18) and they began to acclaim Him, 'Hail, King of the Jews!' (19) They kept beating His head with a reed, and spitting on Him, and kneeling and bowing before Him. (20) After they had mocked Him, they took the purple robe off Him and put His own garments on Him. And they led Him out to crucify Him." *(See also Luke 23:35-37)*

[249] **John 15:13**. "Greater love has no one than this, that one lay down his life for his friends." **Romans 5**. "(7) For one will hardly die for a righteous man; though perhaps for the good man someone would dare even to die. (8) But God demonstrates His own love toward us, in that while we were yet sinners, Christ died for us."

Now after Christ died

He was placed in a tomb,[250]

Which first was a grave,

but then served as a womb,

Travailing and quaking[251]

the day He was raised[252]

And brought forth by God

to be handled and praised.[253]

The Firstborn from death[254]

on that day emerged He

With power to save

to the utmost degree.[255]

---

[250]**Mark 15:46**. "Joseph bought a linen cloth, took Him down, wrapped Him in the linen cloth and laid Him in a tomb which had been hewn out in the rock; and he rolled a stone against the entrance of the tomb."

[251]**Matthew 28:2**. "And behold, a severe earthquake had occurred, for an angel of the Lord descended from heaven and came and rolled away the stone and sat upon it."

[252]**1 Corinthians 15:4**. " . . . He was raised on the third day according to the Scriptures,"

[253]**Luke 24:39**. " . . . touch Me and see, for a spirit does not have flesh and bones as you see that I have." **John 20**. "(27) Then He said to Thomas, 'Reach here with your finger and see My hands; and reach here your hand and put it into My side . . . .' (28) Thomas answered and said to Him, 'My Lord and my God!'"

[254]**Colossians 1:18**. "He is . . . the firstborn from the dead . . . ."

[255]**Hebrews 7:25**. "Therefore He is also able to save to the uttermost those who come to God through Him, since He always lives to make intercession for them." *(New King James Version)*

At God's own right hand

    Christ now reigns from on high,[256]

A Friend in high places

    to sinners[257] who cry[258]

To Him for forgiveness,

    their evils confessed.

He gives them a pardon

    and then makes them blessed.[259]

As Prince He is Savior[260]

    to all who believe,[261]

Who come to Him humbly

    His grace to receive.

---

[256]**Ephesians 1.** "(20) . . . He [God] raised Him [Jesus] from the dead, and seated Him at His right hand in the heavenly places, (21) far above all rule and authority and power and dominion, and every name that is named, not only in this age, but also in the one to come."

[257]**1 Timothy 1:15.** ". . . Christ Jesus came into the world to save sinners . . . ."

[258]**Romans 10:13.** "for whosoever will call on the name of the Lord will be saved."

[259]**Romans 10:12.** ". . . the same Lord is Lord of all, abounding in riches for all who call on Him;"

[260]**Acts 5:31.** "He [Jesus] is the One whom God exalted to His right hand as a Prince and a Savior, to grant repentance . . . and forgiveness of sins."

[261]**Ephesians 2.** "(8) For by grace you have been saved through faith; and that not of yourselves, it is the gift of God; (9) not as a result of works, so that no one may boast."

Now when my time came

and to Jesus I cried,

He gave me the pardon[262]

for which I had sighed,

He cleansed me completely

from wrongs I had done,[263]

Released me from bondage

to sins, ev'ry one.

He shattered sin's chains

which had held me before,

And thus made me free

not to sin any more.[264]

---

[262]**Ephesians 1:7**. "In Him we have redemption through His blood, the forgiveness of our trespasses, according to the riches of His grace."

[263]**1 Corinthians 6**. "(9) Or do you not know that the unrighteous shall not inherit the kingdom of God? Do not be deceived; neither fornicators, nor idolaters, nor adulterers, nor effeminate, nor homosexuals, (10) nor thieves, nor the covetous, nor drunkards, nor revilers, nor swindlers, will inherit the kingdom of God. (11) Such were some of you; but you were washed . . . ."

[264]**Romans 6**. "(6) knowing this, that our old self was crucified with Him, in order that our body of sin might be done away with, so that we would no longer be slaves to sin; (7) for he who has died is freed from sin. . . . (14) For sin shall not be master over you, for you are not under law but under grace."

A child of the Father

He made me to be[265]

And gave me the Spirit

as His guarantee[266]

That, being God's child,

I will one day obtain

A heavenly treasure

that never will wane.[267]

While in me, the Spirit

gives power[268] and love[269]

And sweet premonitions

of glory above.[270]

---

[265]**Ephesians 1:5.** "He predestined us to adoption as sons through Jesus Christ to Himself . . . ."

[266]**Ephesians 1.** "(13) . . . you were sealed in Him with the Holy Spirit of promise, (14) who is given as a pledge of our inheritance. . ."

[267]**1 Peter 1.** "(3) Blessed be . . . God . . . who . . . has caused us to be born again to a living hope . . . (4) to obtain an inheritance which is imperishable and undefiled and will not fade away, reserved in heaven for you,"

[268]**Acts 1:8.** ". . . you will receive power when the Holy Spirit has come upon you." **Ephesians 3:16.** "that He would grant you . . . to be strengthened with power through His Spirit in the inner man,"

[269]**Romans 5:5.** " . . . the love of God has been poured out within our hearts through the Holy Spirit . . ."

[270]**Romans 8.** "(16) The Spirit Himself testifies with our spirit that we are children of God, (17) and if children, heirs also, heirs of God and fellow heirs with Christ. . . . (23) . . . we ourselves, having the first fruits of the Spirit, even we ourselves groan within ourselves, waiting eagerly for our adoption as sons, the redemption of our body."

In saving, God also
did justify me,[271]
Accounting me righteous
by His own decree,[272]
Declaring me guiltless
of all of my sin,
And bringing His wrath
against me to an end.[273]
This wrath Christ appeased[274]
in full brunt on the Tree,
When, bearing my sin,
He endured it for me.[275]

---

[271]**Romans 5:1**. "Therefore, having been justified by faith, we have peace with God through our Lord Jesus Christ,"

[272]**Romans 4:5**. "But to the one who does not work, but believes in Him who justifies the ungodly, his faith is credited as righteousness,"

[273]**1 Thessalonians 5:9**. "For God has not destined us for wrath, but for obtaining salvation through our Lord Jesus Christ,"

[274]**1 John 2:2**. ". . . He [Christ] Himself is the propitiation for our sins . . . ." ('propitiation' = satisfaction, appeasement of wrath)

[275]**1 Peter 2:24**. " . . . He Himself bore our sins in His body on the tree . . . ." (literal translation)

So now God relates
    to me only with grace,[276]
The former wrath banished
    without any trace![277]
And each day I'm made
    a bit more as I should,
His grace using all things
    to render me good.[278]
Yes, even in trials
    God's grace abounds too
And does me the good
    He assigns it to do.[279]

---

[276]**Romans 5:21.** " . . . as sin reigned in death, even so grace would reign through righteousness *[justification]* . . . ."

[277]**Romans 5:9.** "Much more then, having now been justified by His blood, we shall be saved from the wrath of God through Him."

[278]**Romans 8:28.** "And we know that God causes all things to work together for good to those who love God, to those who are called according to His purpose."

[279]**Romans 5.** "(1) Therefore, having been justified by faith, we have peace with God through our Lord Jesus Christ, (2) through whom also we have obtained our introduction by faith into this grace in which we stand; and we exult in hope of the glory of God. (3) And not only this, but we also exult in our tribulations, knowing that tribulation brings about perseverance; (4) and perseverance, proven character; and proven character, hope; (5) and hope does not disappoint, because the love of God has been poured out within our hearts through the Holy Spirit who was given to us."

And when I am sinning

    God's grace does abound,[280]

Ensuring my justified

    status is sound.

No wrath is awakened

    in God at my sin,

Because Christ appeased it[281]

    (to say so again).

God's heart pulses only

    with passionate grace,

Which jealously wants me

    back in His embrace.[282]

---

[280]**Romans.** "(5:20) . . . where sin increased, grace abounded all the more, (21) so that, as sin reigned in death, even so grace would reign through righteousness to eternal life through Jesus Christ our Lord. (6:1) What shall we say then? Are we to continue in sin so that grace may increase?"

[281]**1 John 2:2.** ". . . He [Christ] Himself is the propitiation for our sins . . . ." ('propitiation' = satisfaction, appeasement of wrath)

[282]**James 4:5.** "Or do you suppose that the Scripture is speaking to no purpose that says, The Spirit Whom He has caused to dwell in us yearns over us – and He yearns for the Spirit [to be welcome] – with a jealous love." *(The Amplified Bible)*

God does not require
  even that I confess,
Before He desires
  His forgiveness to press.
Forgiveness has been
  in His heart all along;
And when I approach Him
  to make right my wrong,
He runs up to greet me
  and draws to me near,[283]
Embracing and kissing[284]
  and ready to clear.[285]

---

[283]**James 4:8.** "Draw near to God and He will draw near to you . . . ."

[284]**Luke 15.** "(20) So he got up and came to his father. But while he was still a long way off, his father saw him and felt compassion for him, and ran and embraced him and kissed him. (21) And the son said to him, 'Father, I have sinned against heaven and in your sight; I am no longer worthy to be called your son.' (22) But the father said to his slaves, 'Quickly bring out the best robe and put it on him, and put a ring on his hand and sandals on his feet; (23) and bring the fattened calf, kill it, and let us eat and celebrate; (24) for this son of mine was dead and has come to life again; he was lost and has been found.' And they began to celebrate."

[285]**1 John 1:9.** "If we confess our sins, He is faithful and righteous to forgive us our sins and to cleanse us from all unrighteousness."

God does see my sins

and He grieves at them so,[286]

For when I am sinning,

His love I don't know.[287]

He even will send me

some heart-rending pain,

So I'll learn new ways

and His holiness gain.

His disciplines always

are with love imbued,[288]

A love that seeks ever

my ultimate good.

---

[286]**Ephesians 4:30.** "Do not grieve the Holy Spirit of God . . . ."

[287]**John 15:10.** "If you keep My commandments, you will abide in My love . . . ." (*Jesus' words imply that if I don't keep God's commandments, then I am not fully abiding in His love while sinning.*)

[288]**Hebrews 12.** "(7) It is for discipline that you endure; God deals with you as with sons; for what son is there whom his father does not discipline? (8) But if you are without discipline, of which we all have become partakers, then you are illegitimate children and not sons. (9) Furthermore, we had earthy fathers to discipline us, and we respected them; shall we not much rather be subject to the Father of spirits, and live? (10) For they disciplined us for a short time as seemed best to them, but He disciplines us for our good, so that we may share His holiness."

So this is my story;

   ongoing it is.

How shall I thank God

   for this gospel of His?

A gift that keeps giving,[289]

   the gospel confers

The bounty of heaven

   each time I rehearse.

Deserve it? I don't

   on my holiest day;

But this is salvation,

   and herein I'll stay.[290]

---

[289]**Colossians 1**. "(5) . . . the gospel, (6) which has come to you . . . is constantly bearing fruit and increasing . . . since the day you heard of it and understood the grace of God in truth;" **Acts 20:32**. ". . . the message of His grace [the gospel] . . . is continually able to build you up and give you the inheritance among all those who are sanctified." *(literal translation)*

[290]**1 Peter 5:12**. ". . . this is the true grace of God. Stand firm in it!" **1 Corinthians 16:13**. ". . . stand firm in the faith . . . ." **Colossians 1**. "(22) . . . He has now reconciled you in His fleshly body through death, in order to present you before Him holy and blameless and beyond reproach – (23) if indeed you continue in the faith firmly established and steadfast, and not moved away from the hope of the gospel . . . ."

PART IV

Surprised by the Gospel

The Story Behind the Primer

Terror accomplishes no real obedience.
Suspense brings forth no fruit unto holiness.
No gloomy uncertainty as to God's favor
can subdue one lust,
or correct our crookedness of will.
But the free pardon of the cross uproots sin,
and withers all its branches.
Only the certainty of love,
forgiving love,
can do this.

Horatius Bonar, from *"God's Way of Holiness"*

Surprised by the Gospel

"I've had it!" my heart fumed as I drove home from work that fateful day in the spring of 2001. *"I can't keep going like this!"*

Those driving behind me and beside me on the freeway would have observed nothing out of the ordinary in my driving. They could not have known that I was perilously close to wrecking what was left of my faith. Frustrated by the exhausting task of staying in God's good favor, I was careening away from God once again.

Indeed, I was a believer in Christ. In fact, a number of times throughout my life I had prayed to God, putting my trust in Christ and asking Him to save me. Baptized at the age of five, and again at the age of fifteen, I would have been baptized yet again at the age of seventeen were it not for the protestations of my pastor. My problem was certainly not a lack of faith or professions of faith. My problem was that I couldn't seem to figure out how to stay in the good favor of the God who had saved me.

Laboring Over My Justification

I would never have acknowledged this to be the case at the time, but I labored for most of my life to maintain my justified status before God, and I was always left frustrated in my attempts to do so. The "God" I believed in was frequently angered at me. When I would come into His presence to make right some wrong, His arms were tightly folded, and His eyes were slow to meet mine. I imagined an angry look on His face, and it was always up to me to figure out some way to mollify Him.

I figured that if I beat myself up sufficiently in His presence, or pled with Him long enough, or just waited a few hours to put a little distance between me and my sin, then He might warm to me again.

This view of God would work for a short while, but eventually the sheer quantity of times I failed God would reach a threshold where I was convinced that He was fed up with me. I also grew weary of always falling out of His favor and having to confess or work my way back into His good graces. Exhausted from such efforts, I would eventually give up trying to relate to God at all.

I would then go weeks and months where all I did was simply try not to do anything too stupid or overtly sinful. But inwardly I often harbored much sin; and, eventually, I would find myself acting out in ways that would frighten me and bring the Spirit's conviction upon me. Feeling convicted over such sin, I would return to God as a prodigal and renew my efforts to please Him this time around. With a burst of energy, I would throw myself into trying to relate to God once again, only to end up a short time later exactly as I had so many times before: frustrated, fed up, and exhausted.

I operated this way through college and seminary, and even through the first decade of my ministry as a pastor. All the while, I hung onto my faith, because I knew something better was available. I just didn't know how to get to it. God was gracious to teach me many things along the way that continued to move me forward, but rest in Christ eluded me.

The Final Straw

In April of 2001, I was in the fourth week of a season of renewal in my walk with the Lord. I was relating to God with renewed passion and was experiencing significant growth as a result. But the same wearisome agitation began to grow over me as the days wore by, and it was wearing me to a nub.

Driving home from work one day, my mind came back to the Lord after I had allowed my thoughts to drift for about ten minutes. I was instantly concerned about what I might have just been thinking about in the previous ten minutes. *"Have I been thinking anything sinful?"* I asked myself. *"If so, then God would be angry at me for letting my thoughts wander so. Or maybe I wasn't even thinking sinful thoughts, but perhaps God is upset with me because I wasn't thinking on Him instead."*

My mind began to agitate, and I winced under the Lord's gaze. *"Lord, are we OK?"* I asked. *"Have I thought any thoughts that have offended You? Do I need to make anything right in order to restore our relationship?"*

I anxiously retraced my thoughts from the previous ten minutes. I felt I needed to do this in order to know the countenance of God towards me at that moment. If He was angry, then I had to get back into His good graces.

A feeling of nausea began to sweep over me, and years of pent-up frustration seemed to coalesce in that one moment. *"Surely, relating to God can't be this difficult!"* my heart screamed. *"Why is it so hard to stay in His good graces? I can't keep track of every thought in order to make sure that He stays favorably disposed towards me! This isn't possible!"*

Feeling exhausted at the thought of a lifetime of having to tend so obsessively to keeping myself in the good favor of God, I felt a manic urge to trash the whole effort.

The words of a hymn came to my mind and I began to sing them: *"Jesus, I am resting, resting, in the joy of what Thou art . . . ."* As I sang the words, I agonized over the fact that my own experience was far removed from the rest about which the songwriter spoke.

When I got home, I found that my wife and kids were not at home. So I grabbed my Bible and began reading Romans 5 out loud as I paced the floor in our living room. What led me to Romans 5 I don't recall. But I'm glad I landed there, because the chapter saved my life.

I started reading: "*Therefore, having been justified by faith, we have peace with God through our Lord Jesus Christ, through whom also we have obtained our introduction by faith into this grace in which we stand. And we exult . . . .*"

As I continued through the chapter, my soul was stirred by the inspired exultations of a man who rejoiced in, rather than worried about, his justified status before God. This justification brought him into a gracious standing with God that was accomplished and always maintained by Jesus Christ.

The more I read, the more I began to see something I had not seen before. As a justified one, I am under God's gracious favor at all times because of what Jesus did! This favored standing with God has nothing to do with my performance, but only with the performance of Jesus! As I read through the length of the chapter, I began to see that my justification was not something to agitate over, but to exult in, not something to wrestle for, but to rest in. I stole a glimpse into chapter 6 and realized that even when I sin, God's grace abounds to me all the more as He graciously maintains my justified status.

The above realizations may seem like no-brainers to some, but Paul's teaching on justification hit me that day as never before. Indeed, I had always believed I was justified, but I guess I treated my justification as some sort of legal fiction that had little direct bearing on the mechanics of how God related to me and how I related to Him. I suppose I would have imagined God saying, "*Yeah, technically you're justified, but I'm angry with you anyway for what you did today!*"

But now I realized that absolutely 100% of the wrath I deserve for my sins was truly spent on Jesus, and there is none of God's anger left over for me to bear, even when I fail God as a Christian. Hence, God now has only love, compassion, and deepest affection for me, and this love is without any admixture of wrath whatsoever. God always looks upon me and treats me with gracious favor, always seeking to work all things together for my ultimate and eternal good. All of these realities hold true even when I sin.

Being justified in Christ doesn't mean that God no longer sees or cares about my sin. He does see, and He is grieved by my sin. But His gracious favor upon me remains utterly unchanged by my sin, and no wrath is awakened in Him against me – because Christ already bore it all! In fact, God favors me so much when I sin that He sends chastisement into my life. He does so because He is for me, and He loves me, and He disciplines me for my ultimate good.

Drinking in the Good News

Over the next few days, I wrote out some truths regarding my justification on a 3x5 card, and I carried that card around with me everywhere I went. I would pull the card out and read it several times a day. As I did so, I could hardly believe my good fortune. I drank in the doctrine of my justification like a thirsty man drinking a tall glass of water in the desert. The way those truths put my soul at rest was indescribable.

So delicious was the good news regarding my justification that I began to fear that I had misunderstood something. With fear and trembling, I ran what I had learned by two fellow-pastors and by the elders of Cornerstone. I also consulted a few evangelical theology books to make sure I wasn't misunderstanding something. To my great relief, I got a green light from all of these checkpoints! They all confirmed that I was rightly understanding what the Scriptures taught regarding my justification.

I felt like a kid in a candy store. How did I not see these things before? The gospel is the craziest thing I've ever heard in my life. And it's true!

The 3x5 card soon turned into the front side of a half sheet of paper, and one side quickly turned into two. I called it "A Gospel Primer" and kept inserting it into our church's Sunday bulletins to make sure everyone was getting the good news of the gospel. I kept quoting the contents of the Primer to myself in order to remain mindful of the grace of God in which I stood, because I found it too easy to get out of "gospel mode" and fall back into a performance-based relationship with God. Eventually, the single-page primer turned into a book, now entitled, A Gospel Primer for Christians.

Released from the burden of having to maintain my righteous standing with God, I quickly found that I had enormous amounts of passion to put into growing in holiness and ministering God's amazing grace to other people. I had never had such energy available for ministry before, because so much of it was consumed with tending to my standing before God. I also found the grace of the gospel producing in me a huge passion to love and obey God. In moments of temptation, I enjoyed saying to myself, "*You know, I can commit this sin, and God's grace would abound to me all the more as He maintains my justified status. . . . But it is precisely for this reason that I choose not to commit this sin!*" In such moments I would walk away from sin with laughter in my heart.

96

Amazing Grace!

Indeed, I still struggle with sin, and I daily fall short of what I know God wants from me. But without question, the Lord allowed me to turn a significant corner in the spring of 2001. There are still many areas of my life that I have not yet brought the gospel fully to bear upon. And I am still learning and growing in my experience of the fullness of the gospel. But, as exciting as what I've already learned is, I see Jesus standing before me saying, "*There is more.*"

And to me, a hell-deserving sinner, that's just plain crazy. God's grace is amazing!

About the Author

❧

Milton Vincent (B.A., Bob Jones University; M.Div., The Master's Seminary) formerly taught English Grammar and served as a Faculty Associate of Old Testament Language and Literature at The Master's Seminary in Sun Valley, California. Since January of 1992, he has been serving as the Pastor-Teacher of Cornerstone Fellowship Bible Church in Riverside, California. He and his wife, Donna, live in the Riverside area with their four children.